D0484436

LIBERAL
ANXIETIES
and
LIBERAL
EDUCATION

THE ANNUAL NEW YORK REVIEW OF BOOKS

AND

HILL AND WANG

LECTURE SERIES

Series No. 1
given in Berkeley
in 1994

Also by Alan Ryan

The Philosophy of John Stuart Mill
The Philosophy of the Social Sciences
J. S. Mill
Property and Political Theory
Property
Bertrand Russell: A Political Life
John Dewey and the High Tide of American Liberalism

LIBERAL
ANXIETIES
and
LIBERAL
EDUCATION

Alan Ryan

HILL AND WANG

A DIVISION OF FARRAR, STRAUS AND GIROUX

NEW YORK

Hill and Wang
A division of Farrar, Straus and Giroux
19 Union Square West, New York 10003

Copyright © 1998 by Alan Ryan
All rights reserved
Distributed in Canada by Douglas & McIntyre Ltd.
Printed in the United States of America
Designed by Peter Buchanan-Smith
First edition, 1998

Library of Congress Cataloging-in-Publication Data
Ryan, Alan.
    Liberal anxieties and liberal education / Alan Ryan. — 1st ed.
        p.   cm. — (The annual New York review of books and Hill
and Wang lecture series ; ser. no. 1)
    Includes bibliographical references and index.
    ISBN 0-8090-6539-8 (alk. paper)
    1. Education, Humanistic. 2. Education, Humanistic—United
States—Philosophy. 3. Liberalism. 4. Liberalism—United States.
5. Education, Higher—Philosophy. 6. Education, Higher—United
States—Philosophy. I. Title. II. Series.
LC1011.R93   1998
370.11'2—dc21   97-38930
                                                              CIP

CONTENTS

CONCORDIA UNIVERSITY LIBRARY
PORTLAND. OR 97211

ACKNOWLEDGMENTS

This short book began three years ago as a series of lectures at the Townsend Center of the University of California at Berkeley, and it preserves the informal and conversational tone of those lectures. I have since thought a good deal about what I left unsaid then, and about how best to respond to the kindly but searching questions that Professors Judith Butler, David Hollinger, Troy Duster, and Sheldon Rothblatt put to me in the colloquium that followed the lectures. I thank Bliss Carnochan and the many members of my audience whose names I do not know for their questions, doubts, and objections; and Tom Laqueur, Tina Gillis, and the Townsend Center for their hospitality. I tried out early versions of chapters 2 and 3 as the Whidden Lecturer at McMaster University in November 1993, and I am grateful to Professors Les King, Richard Rempel, Louis Greenspan, and my audiences there for their friendly and critical attention. In my last revisions, I have had the invaluable help of Robert Silvers of *The New York Review of Books*, under whose auspices the lectures were given, and of Elisabeth Sifton, who is responsible for their present publication.

LIBERAL
ANXIETIES
and
LIBERAL
EDUCATION

INTRODUCTION

For some months, the notice board of a church outside Princeton, New Jersey, sported a slogan long familiar to me: "Philosophers have interpreted the world. We must change it." I have wondered whether the minister who put those words there knew their origins in Karl Marx's *Theses on Feuerbach* (the eleventh thesis runs, "Philosophers have interpreted the world in various ways; the point, however, is to change it"), and, if so, what his congregation thought about that. The fact that a slogan from the atheist Marx could be so easily borrowed by a Baptist minister shows how the quick, dismissive contrast between the interpreter and the activist, the scholar and the doer, can be found all over the intellectual, moral, and political landscape. ("Those who can, do; those who can't, teach.") In case anyone picks up this book looking for detailed instructions on how to change the educational practices of the United States and the rest of the Western world, I should forestall disappointment: before we can change the world—before we can change it intelligently, at least—we must understand it. What follows contains much about what decent schools and colleges are (or would be) like, what they teach (or would teach), and how they (would) do it. It contains no magic formulas for the creation of such schools and colleges, let alone for what governments and the public—

on both sides of the Atlantic—really want, which is to have large numbers of them at no cost. There are no magic formulas. Not all the things that we want from our educational system are consistent with each other, and much of what follows explains why. Some, though by no means all, good education is expensive. Even worse, the most important changes must take place outside schools and colleges if these institutions are to do their work successfully.

American education at every level needs change, and some of the change must be dramatic. It is an obvious and much commented on disgrace that American teenagers perennially score well down in the rankings in international tests of simple mathematical and linguistic competence, and much lower than the students of far poorer countries;[1] it is also a disgrace, though a less obvious one, that most humanities graduates from "good" colleges would be hard-pressed to detect simple fallacies of statistical reasoning and that their colleagues in the sciences and mathematics would be hard-pressed to explain those fallacies in a paragraph of clear English prose. A recent writer began a history of American higher education with the observation that "criticizing colleges has always amounted to something of a national pastime, dating back practically to the colonial era. Yet in the waning years of the twentieth century, public disaffection with American higher education seems to have generated a cacophony of public criticism almost without historical precedent."[2] He went on to supply a long list of rather solid reasons for such disaffection, ranging from a national graduation rate that sees barely 50 percent of students emerge with a diploma after five years to alarming statistics about the absence of mathematics, foreign languages, history, and literature from the transcripts of many of those who do graduate. Given these inadequacies, it is hardly surprising, though it is surely disgraceful, that so few students feel any sense of "ownership" about their country's history, let alone about the human race's achievements in the arts and sciences, and its diverse religious and cultural attachments.

Debates over higher education have been strikingly acrimonious, but the elementary school curriculum has perhaps attracted more consistent and continuous attention, as it recently has in E. D. Hirsch's books from *Cultural Literacy* to *The Schools We Need*.[3] Since my own life has been spent in universities—the excellence of whose educational efforts Professor Hirsch takes entirely too much for granted—I concentrate on what happens there, and write mostly about pre-college education from that standpoint. It would be foolish and thoroughly offensive to do so without acknowledging that elementary and high schools exist for many more purposes than to prepare students for college. Although something over 40 percent of American high school graduates go on to some form of college education, the dropout rate at every level below the very best means that even now three Americans in four are employed with no more than a high school diploma to their names.

But low college graduation rates are not the main source of our current anxieties. In the United States, as in Great Britain and Europe, the condition of inner-city schools at all levels causes the most anxiety, and their failures seem the most resistant to improvement. Since my subject is what nineteenth- and twentieth-century liberals have wanted from education at its best, I concentrate on the virtues and shortcomings of the best education that the United States and Britain have to offer. But the situation of the truly educationally disadvantaged is a worse problem in terms of sheer human misery than any I shall address. It is a diversion (but a necessary one) to explain briefly why their plight is worse than anything I shall discuss, but also why it is not my subject even so.

To recognize that the condition of so-called sink schools is simply appalling is not to adopt one view of education rather than another, and particularly not to adopt any of the disputable views I shall discuss and defend. To acknowledge the disastrousness of such schools is only to recognize that over the past thirty years the lives of the prosperous and the lives of the poor have become more and more separate, and that the destructive effects of technological and economic changes on unskilled inner-city dwellers have thus far defeated all our attempts to palliate them. The inner-city sink school—the school where nobody wants to teach, where nobody wants to study, and where students float in and out because their parents are perpetually on the edge of homelessness or worse—is a problem that has to be solved in more ways than we know how to deal with. It is not only the school that needs fixing but the community, and not only the community but the wider economy, whose impact on the community is the source of its disasters. Ultimately, of course, we are faced with a political system maladapted to the tasks it confronts. The one question that the dreadful condition of such schools does not raise is the purpose of education at its best.

INTRODUCTION

The Politics of Education

Jonathan Kozol's *Illiterate America* provides some terrifying, but uncontroversial, statistics that can usefully illustrate my point: "Twenty-five million Americans cannot read the poison warnings on a can of pesticide, a letter from their child's teacher, or the front page of a daily paper. An additional 35 million read only at a level which is less than equal to the full survival needs of our society . . . Sixteen percent of white adults, 44 percent of blacks, and 56 percent of Hispanic citizens are functional or marginal illiterates."[4] This was written in 1985. In the past decade, things have, if anything, gotten slightly worse for the black and Hispanic population. The "report cards" that several states, including New York and New Jersey, have now started to produce for each school paint grim pictures—a decade-long record of small gains against a background of larger failures. President George Bush's boast that by the year 2000 American education was going to be the best in the world still looks like a bad joke for the children of Newark, or Camden, or Washington Heights.

It is a commonplace that substantial improvement in the economic lot of the disadvantaged is politically impossible; and it is arguable, though I believe false, that it is economically impossible. But much more narrowly educational changes are also blocked, even when they would help all schools, and inner-city schools more than most. The unwillingness of voters to pay higher taxes for improved public services is not the most important obstacle, for changes that cost scarcely anything are also blocked by American partisan politics. One essential and long-overdue change in the United States is the establishment of clear national standards for student attainment at various ages from six to eighteen. Nobody believes that an "A student" is the same excellent scholar in every school in the country, and everybody knows that an objective test of student attainment would reveal quite painfully just how different the standards are in different schools. Even in the absence of such a national system, SAT scores reveal some of the truth about college-bound students. During recent arguments about the abolition of race-based affirmative action in California, admissions officers at Berkeley claimed that almost all their applicants were "straight A" students in high school. Yet the average SATs of entering students at Berkeley were more than two hundred points lower than those of entering students at Harvard—many of whom would have been B+ or A− students at tougher high schools. But setting up a national examination system, which implies at least some minimal national curriculum common to all schools in the country, is at odds with the current hostility to, and skepticism of, central government. The Republican Party's "Contract with America," on which the party fought and won the 1994 Congressional elections, proposed to abolish the Department of Education entirely; the Democratic Party has for the past decade run away from the label of "the party of big government." If either party tried to do anything serious about setting national standards, it would be ambushed by the other. There are glimmerings of hope in some states. Governor Christine Todd Whitman has recently pushed through a statewide curriculum for New Jersey, and it may be that when she ceases to be governor her successor will continue to take an interest in the matter, and that real progress will be made. It would be unwise to bet on it, and in the meantime the absence of a permanent national standard remains a scandal.

The loss to students in inner-city schools is greater than it is to their more fortunate peers. It is these students who are likely to be intermittent attendees, who have to drop into strange classes and strange courses as their parents—or more often only their mothers—move from one place to another. There is little that curricular reform can do about such social dislocation, but an agreed, minimal national curriculum would at least mean that students could migrate from one school to another without having to start from scratch on each occasion. Conversely, teachers would be able to assume that some of the material they were trying to teach was familiar to new students.

In Britain a national curriculum was instituted in 1983, in the teeth of universal skepticism or hostility from teachers but with the cautious support of most parents. It has undoubtedly had many bad side effects: by the time a school has scheduled the lesson periods that are required to cover the syllabi for the "Key Stage" assessments (national tests at the equivalent of American ninth grade) there is precious little room for anything else. Teachers complain, rightly, that when school performance is assessed in terms of the national curriculum, politicians are tempted to use "league tables" (national rankings of success in exam results) for party political purposes rather than as a tool to improve schools. If a national curriculum were instituted in the United States, it is hard to believe that Republican governors would be absolutely fastidious in resisting the temptation to denounce inner-city school boards that had from time immemorial provided sinecures for Democratic loyalists. Making political capital out of bad results is easier than improving the schools. The new common curriculum that Governor Whitman seduced her legislators into agreeing to in December 1996 is vulnerable to the complaints leveled against the British national curriculum. In particular, it is difficult to accommodate extra foreign languages and an in-depth education in the arts within such a framework. Overall, however, it has worked well in Britain and is likely to do so in New Jersey. Not the least of its merits is that it makes it possible to assess a school's success against an agreed-upon benchmark. I am a trustee of a very large (by British standards) high school near Oxford, and I have watched the school's morale rise as the percentage of children reaching the national benchmarks in English, mathematics, and history has risen. Nor has the effect been confined to assessment under the national curriculum; the level of performance in national academic examinations has risen equally sharply, and so has the number of students remaining at school to take advanced qualifications. It goes without saying that there is much that has not improved —a national curriculum does little to inspire ambition at the top.

The fate of recent attempts to create a national history curriculum on the two sides of the Atlantic may be instructive. In Britain, there was a heated argument about what should be included and what not, and a rather less heated debate about the balance to be expected between factual knowledge and an understanding of historical method. Since everyone concerned knew that the government was determined that some syllabus rather than none was to be instituted, the argument had to come to a conclusion and it did. Some concessions were made to critics of traditional political history—parodied as "Kings and Queens of England and a list of notable battles"—but a rather straightforward national curriculum was established. In the United States, a semiofficial working party with no great political weight created the curriculum. The working party fell into the familiar trap of trying too hard to redress the biases of old-fashioned political history, replacing them with the biases of the "new social history." The result was a syllabus that dealt at length with the victims of American colonialism and with the lives of previously unnoticed Americans, and rather briefly with Jefferson, Washington, and the heroes of the more usual sort of political history. Unsurprisingly, Lynne Cheney, the former head of the National Endowment for the Humanities, who had spent the previous fifteen years attacking what she thought of as radical corruptions of the American intellectual tradition, denounced their work. It was, she said, little more than an attempt to warp the minds of the young by telling them a series of half-truths and untruths calculated to turn them into unpatriotic and antisocial renegades.

There could have been a useful public discussion about how much history and what kind American school students could learn; instead, there was a shouting match. No one, sadly, drew the obvious moral: that in the absence of the kind of government direction that characterizes European countries and Britain, national standards can only be created consensually. They must be built around a minimally agreed-upon factual content, a little methodological instruction, and not much more. It is sufficient, however; on such a basis, individual schools, and individual teachers within schools, can properly strike out in different directions. If every sixteen-year-old student could draw a simple time line of the major events in the Civil War from the first shots at Fort Sumter to the surrender at Appomattox Court House, we might safely leave it to the students and their teachers to consider whether John Brown was a hero or a half-crazed fanatic, and whether Lincoln was as reluctant as he claimed to be to take the last steps to emancipation. And by the same token, if every sixteen-year-old student could provide a one-paragraph account of what Charles Darwin discovered and why it mattered, we might leave it to the students and their teachers to argue among themselves about the impact of Darwin on the credibility of the Book of Genesis—or not, as they chose. Even a minimal syllabus could achieve the respect for the difference between fact and myth that Americans are so reluctant to acknowledge. What is unspeakable is to accept in the name of choice that Christian academies may teach complete nonsense in place of biology and Afrocentric schools absurdities in place of African history.

We have, as such examples suggest, recently been too angry to think clearly. A dozen books a week have appeared, denouncing the shortcomings of our schools and colleges, the failures of their students and their students' teachers, and by the same token the foolishness of the remedies offered by all the commentators on the opposite side of the political, religious, and cultural divides of the day. If shouting could improve American education, our young people would be geniuses. Public education is at the mercy of cultural, political, and economic forces that teachers and administrators can do little about, and these forces are not confined to public education. Even the best-financed private schools and colleges are not immune to the strains of the wider culture—as every report of well-heeled young people being expelled from Groton or Exeter for smoking pot reminds the students' anxious parents, and as every suicide by an unhappy Harvard student reminds the anxious deans and tutors. All the same, the impact of social, political, and economic change falls very differently upon the better- and the worse-off.

Public education in affluent American suburbs is not usefully described as in a state of crisis. The education of prosperous middle-class children is intellectually and culturally unambitious, but it equips them to go to college, and to earn a living. This is far from true for the poorest 10 percent of the population. It is particularly far from true when the poorest 10 percent is black and Hispanic. There surely is a crisis of public education in America's ghettos, but it is not an educational crisis. It is part of a much wider crisis: America is an increasingly inegalitarian society, whose inner-city inhabitants have become economically redundant. They are too few in number and too disheveled and disorganized to be politically dangerous, and all the evidence is that most voters would rather pay to incarcerate young men at $30,000 a year than pay whatever it takes to prevent their growing up to a life of crime. (This is not wholly irrational; given past failures, taxpayers must in any event pay to incarcerate the present generation of felons, so the $7,500 per child per year that it is said to cost to deal with antisocial children is an additional investment.) "If America has any civic standards," writes Theodore Sizer, liberal education theorist and chairman of the Coalition of Essential Schools, "two of the most important are fairness and generosity. Both of these are mocked by the practice of American education."[5] That may not be how most people see it. Americans are certainly generous, but only to those who suffer through no fault of their own; their notions about fairness include the thought that those who receive help should do something to deserve it. Faced with endless television and newspaper reports on the violence, illegitimacy, and alienation that rack the worst areas of Chicago, Los Angeles, Washington, New York, and Detroit, not to mention the more sophisticated analyses in works such as Charles Murray's *Losing Ground*, the respectable can hardly be blamed for thinking that increasing the budgets of failing school districts is not generosity but pouring resources into a bottomless pit.

For a discussion of liberal education and its purpose (which this book is), the point about the horrors of inner-city schools is how little they have to do with educational theory. If every student in America went to a clean, sanitary, nonviolent, and well-managed middle-class high school in a quiet midwestern suburb, if none of the young women had babies before they graduated and none of the young men went to jail, there would still be educational theorists and political philosophers standing on the sidelines complaining that these respectable young people emerged as bland, uncultivated, conformist, unimaginative canon fodder for the industrial, managerial, and service armies of the modern economy. They—I would be one of them—would complain that the students' souls had not been seared by Dostoyevsky, their imaginations not liberated by reading Baudelaire in French, their analytical capacities not stretched by thermodynamics, and their political aspirations not touched by encountering history teachers with a passion for Eugene Debs. Critics of American society in the 1950s wrote in just such tones. But it has to be said that if we were offered a magic wand that would transform most inner-city high schools into just such bland and boring and suburban places, we should use it. It would be both mad and inhumane to do anything else.

Is there anything special about the horrors of the modern inner city and its schools; were things not equally bad a century ago? Did not people a hundred years ago complain as loudly as we do about "race suicide" when they looked at the inner-city poor? The answer is surely that things were in many ways as bad a century ago, but that we are unnerved by something besides urban squalor and violence in themselves. Gustave Doré's etchings of Victorian Whitechapel—a notorious slum in the East End of London—look like vignettes of the lower circles of hell; photographs of New York's Lower East Side at the turn of the century are hardly more attractive. But there was once a long, slow gradation from these lower depths through the environments in which the respectable working class lived and up to the homes of the prosperous and the rich. We know now as contemporaries did not that the degradation was temporary, and that the grandchildren of the slum dwellers would in due course prosper in the suburbs. What distresses us today is, on the one hand, the sharpness of the contrast between the blighted inner city and the prosperity

INTRODUCTION

of suburban America and, on the other, our uncertainty that there is any escape route out of the horrors. *Savage Inequalities* was the title of Kozol's first account of the blighted lives of inner-city children, and both words counted equally in his indictment of the society that allowed such contrasts to exist.

In a vast country, there are innumerable bright spots: parochial schools perform wonders in terrible places, and teacher-administrators of genius, such as Deborah Meier of the East Harlem school, show what can be done in small programs with attentive teachers. But compared with other prosperous, democratically governed societies, the American scene is too often grim. Although it is grim in ways that some European inner cities are beginning to emulate, Sizer is surely right to say that "no other industrial nation in the world tolerates such inequities. No other industrial nation will pay so heavily for their long-range costs. That reality alone should be an embarrassment for Americans."[6] I have already suggested that the long-range costs do not include revolution or civil war; but they do include moral embarrassment and the simple nastiness of living in the kind of society where respectable people fear to travel through the places where their poorer fellow-citizens live. All I have to say about it here is that it is not a reality that it lies within the power of teachers to alter.

Intractable Problems

No matter what curriculum reforms we might put in place, they will make no difference if schools are unsafe and their students distracted by the hazards of daily existence inside and outside their schools. Many thousands of kids come to school each day with knives and even guns in their bags; but it is better gun control and tighter policing that gets guns out of the hands of inner-city teenagers, not peda-gogical theory. Changes in the tenth-grade history syllabus certainly can't do it. This is a platitudinous point, but often overlooked. Nor is it overlooked only by critics who com-plain that schools do not turn out well-behaved and well-educated students under impossible conditions. People working in such conditions who are desperate to achieve *something* naturally overestimate the importance of what they can do. It is this, rather than an irrational affection for far-fetched psychological theories, that has sustained the recent craze for improving students' "self-esteem." Ill-prepared students facing a bleak future can be persuaded to feel good about themselves here and now, even if they have no access to recent textbooks, to decent science lab-oratories, or even to an adequate supply of paper and pens. But however much it improves the climate in the class-room to persuade students to feel good about themselves, it is no substitute for well-equipped laboratories, smaller classes, and newer books.

Above all, what students need is the prospect of decent jobs. Many inner-city high schools suffer 60 percent drop-out rates and graduate only 30 percent of their students before they reach the age of twenty; students know quite well that there are next to no jobs in inner cities that require a high school education. To notice this is not to apportion blame; it is merely to acknowledge a vicious cir-cle. Nobody in his right mind wants to invest in an area where the population is work-shy and illiterate, where

INTRODUCTION

drugs are openly sold in the street and violent crime is commonplace; conversely, nobody in her right mind wants to invest in the self-discipline and hard work required to get a decent education if there is no payoff. Critics of Kozol's accounts of the lives of the children who fill American inner-city schools—*Death at an Early Age*, *Illiterate America*, *Savage Inequalities*, and *Amazing Grace* among them—have sometimes complained that they degenerate into expressions of moral outrage at "society." What else could they do? The scope for old-fashioned self-help on a classroom-by-classroom basis in the South Bronx or Cabrini Green is not great. Teachers, parents, and local school boards can't change the Federal Reserve Board's belief that controlling inflation is its most important task and move the creation of employment to the top of the federal government's list of priorities; nor can they vote the transportation subsidies and zoning laws that would make jobs other than selling drugs on the street corner an option for inner-city youths. National politicians who could make it a priority to rehabilitate the inner cities or to move their inhabitants elsewhere dare not confront a tax-shy public with the unpalatable truth that investment in a more equal and less racially divided America is expensive. The public in turn can hardly be blamed for doubting that politicians are up to the task: it is very far from obvious what the best strategy for rehabilitation is, or how to implement it. When progress is made, it is by exceedingly indirect means. A police policy of "zero tolerance" toward minor infractions reduces the level of more serious crime; a reduction in serious crime encourages shopkeepers to stay in an area. The existence of shops and services encourages the individuals

INTRODUCTION

and agencies who have funds to rehabilitate local housing. Just as there are downward spirals, so there are upward spirals. In the past three years, there seems to have been such an upward spiral in the South Bronx, and it has benefited the schools and the children who attend them. Mayor Rudolph Giuliani's rows with chancellors of the New York City school system have made headlines, and have done nothing to improve the schools; but it may be that the mayor's policing policies have done good for the education system in unintended ways.

The damage done by poverty, broken families, and physically and emotionally dangerous environments can hardly be exaggerated. Recent (and still controversial) studies of the development of the infant brain show that the most serious educational problems can start long before preschool, let alone elementary school. The neural pathways that allow us to see our surroundings, to hear and speak the language of the adults around us, and to understand what they feel, what they want, and how we can deal with them are not fully formed at birth but laid down in the first months and years of life. Once laid down, they are hard to alter, as almost anyone who tries to learn a foreign language after the age of ten discovers. Children must receive most of the mental and physical stimulation that makes them socially cooperative on the one hand and adept learners on the other years before they reach school—much of it by the age of two, and most of it soon after.[7] What are teachers supposed to do when they receive students who are, in the most literal sense, brain-damaged? They cannot prevent children from being born underweight and undernourished, or being injured by parents who have no inkling of the way the first few months of life affect a child's social, emotional, and intellectual potential. A decent national health service would help the first, and an adequate system of perinatal clinics and child care would help the second. It is not teachers who have failed to provide them. Teachers perform small miracles in unpropitious conditions, but they cannot by themselves make the conditions more propitious.

It is often thought that we cannot solve these problems—and many others—because we have lost the moral consensus that once sustained American society. This thought can merely express a rather pointless wish that the antisocial and incompetent would just behave better; but it can also point us to an important truth. Many successful communities are rich in what has been called "moral capital," and those that are not are usually unsuccessful. Societies that are strong on mutual trust can be economically very effective, as the example of Japan shows; conversely, southern Italy and Sicily, where the *camorra* and the *mafia* have long exploited the general climate of mistrust that they also do a good deal to create, are textbook examples of the poverty caused by a lack of moral capital. The fear that urban black communities are chronically short of this moral capital alarms black American conservatives such as Glenn Loury and Thomas Sowell, and frightens the British as they look at Moss Side in Manchester, Handsworth in Birmingham, and Brixton in London. It is not a new fear, and although it is the black inner city that causes it today, it is not intrinsically a racial fear. A hundred years ago, Charles Mayhew alarmed his middle-class English readers by painting a picture of life in the London slums that

INTRODUCTION

Charles Murray or Mickey Kaus might have painted today. Wholesale illegitimacy, families sodden with booze, an aversion to work, and the transmission of antisocial habits from one generation to the next were prominent features of the (white, or, given its unwashed condition, dirty gray) "classic slum."

Some communities were every bit as poor but remained morally intact; and when the external shackles were removed, they prospered. Poor Jewish communities on the Lower East Side in the early years of this century launched an astonishing number of children into successful careers in all fields from business through law to academic life. Those communities had a moral cohesion that made it easier for parents to get their children to take education seriously, for the community as a whole to excite the charitable impulses of their better-off co-religionists, and for parents to be kept up to the mark both by generalized social pressure and by the psychological pressure of their extended families. Irving Howe's memoir *The World of Our Fathers* paints a persuasive picture of just such a background, from which its author eventually migrated into a distinguished career in politics, literature, and education.

The wish that American society as a whole might recapture something of that cohesion is easy to sympathize with. After many years during which American politics was quieter, blander, and more consensual than that of most Western societies, American politics today has become much noisier and more quarrelsome than politics elsewhere in the Western world. All too often politics today means cultural warfare, and defenders of competing ideals of human excellence fight one another along with those who think that all talk of human excellence is antique blather. It might therefore seem that recovering some kind of moral consensus is the first step in getting away from the politics I am here complaining about. Alas, it is not true. On the one hand, America is a very successful pluralistic society, well able to accommodate a wide range of differing beliefs about the point of human existence; on the other hand, there is a far greater degree of moral consensus than appears on the surface. A recent survey of attitudes to welfare, for instance, revealed that people *on* welfare were even more critical of its effects on recipients' willingness to look for work than was the general public. They were as critical of unmarried women who had children on welfare as the general public, and as hostile as the wider public to people who cheated the welfare system. (This is not as surprising as it might seem; although the percentage of Americans receiving financial aid under Aid to Families with Dependent Children (AFDC) or help from the food stamps program is barely in double figures, almost half of all Americans have either had such help at some time or have known family members who have. They have had firsthand evidence of the effects of welfare on morale and of the general level of honesty or dishonesty among recipients.) The difficulty is that this consensus so strongly emphasizes self-help, hard work, and family values, and rests on no very sophisticated understanding of the modern economy; Sizer is not wrong to emphasize Americans' fairness and generosity, but we need to put these virtues in context. And that context is a very individualistic one. Seymour Martin Lipset's recent survey of the social values of developed countries such as Germany, Canada, Japan, Britain, and the United States discovered that the anti-collectivist ethic for which the United States has always been famous remains intact today. It has served the country very well, and for 70 or 80 percent of the population still does; but it is a bad basis on which to persuade the better-off that they are their brothers' keepers.[8]

American politics is largely a tug-of-war between economic interests. There is nothing shameful about this. It is not unduly materialistic to think that the main task of government is to get people to cooperate in producing the means of life by establishing terms for distributing the results that they all find morally acceptable. After the Depression, there was a period of forty years in which those terms shifted in favor of working people and the poor, and it was widely thought that government should ensure that the poor did not do too badly, and that their children were healthy and well enough educated to secure reliable, well-paid employment. Since the mid-1970s, faith in collective provision has waned, and the goal itself has become less popular. People in affluent suburbs feel little obligation to the inner cities; and a graying population feels little sympathy with the plight of the young. Few well-off property tax payers have children in poorly performing public schools; certainly, they do not have children in the sink schools that most need help. They cannot be moved by family feeling.

The pull of simple self-interest—or self-interest and fear together—is not strong either. The old argument that "we must educate our masters"—which was at its simplest no more than the thought that the better-off had better pay for the education of the working class to avoid socialist insurrection and the loss of their own privileges—cuts no ice if the uneducated are apathetic, ill-organized, and live many miles away from the well-defended, gated communities of the well-to-do. The outrage expressed in Christopher Lasch's best-selling book *The Revolt of the Elites* was an impotent outrage for just this reason; the new elite— lawyers, consultants, deal makers of one kind and another —no longer shared the same space as the worse-off, no longer understood what their lives were about, and no longer wanted to help respectable lower-middle-class people in their constant struggle to preserve their way of life. And because they could walk away from the devastation their irresponsibility had caused, all Lasch could do was berate them. The old threats have lost their bite. Even those who would want more government action doubt whether it will work. A 1992 Gallup poll found that only 19 percent of the population believed in the competence of government (as opposed to 75 percent thirty years ago); skepticism about the possibility of successful government action erodes support for public education and public everything else.

The disadvantaged frequently make it less easy to drum up support for policies that might help them; there are too many foul-mouthed, baggy-pants-clad teenagers among them who make observers think of jail rather than college, and too many incompetent teenage mothers, unsure of the paternity of their hapless children, who make spectators think of taking the children off to orphanages rather than spending money on kindergarten. The fact that the disadvantaged are disproportionately black and Hispanic hardly helps. The black middle classes have fled the city for the suburbs along with the white middle classes, and are no longer the natural allies of the black poor. And although it is true enough that the white poor much outnumber the black poor, it is more importantly true that the white middle class outnumbers the black middle class much more dramatically, so that any program to renew the inner city funded from general taxation requires disproportionately white-earned money to be spent on disproportionately non-white kids.

The localism of American politics adds a further twist. Taxpayers who contribute to the well-being of children in other communities want those communities to be responsible and capable of self-help; but the communities most in need are just those that are short on responsibility and bad at self-help. This is not peculiar to education. The contrasts between the best and the worst in American education are as extreme as, and caused in the same way as, the contrasts between the best and the worst in health care, policing, and every other amenity of existence. They have everything to do with the localism of American politics, with changing demographics and a changing economy, and little to do with American attitudes to education in particular.

Education certainly has its own peculiar burdens, however. The public often seeks changes in the education system for symbolic reasons, as if well-scrubbed faces are the outward evidence of well-scrubbed souls. Even the elite confuse cultural sophistication and moral virtue. As distinguished a thinker as Hannah Arendt found it hard to believe that a person whose soul had been touched by Mozart could be a brute in other respects—overlooking Herbert von Karajan's membership in the Nazi Party, Wagner's anti-Semitism, and much evidence of the same sort—and we are all too ready to suppose that a person who has been "properly" educated will be full of all the virtues. But there is an old jingle, "Things would go much better than ever we thought they could, if only the good were clever and if only the clever were good"—which strongly suggests that the beginning of wisdom is to remember that goodness and cleverness do not always go together. Nor for that matter do all the intellectual virtues: patience is not always the ally of imagination, nor an acute eye for historical detail the natural ally of an ability to generalize usefully. Securing a literate and numerate population can certainly be justified as an investment in human capital; indeed, every study suggests that education is both individually and socially an extremely good investment in the simplest monetary terms. What cannot be shown is that it is an investment in ethical terms. The only thing Mozart can be guaranteed to do for those whose souls he touches is to touch their souls.

A Philosophy of Education

This book is about liberal education rather than about vocational education (though I occasionally challenge the distinction), and much of it is therefore about high school and college education rather than "the basics." But the basics are what everything else must rest upon. Indeed, the difference between liberals and conservatives in educational matters for the past two centuries has largely been that conservatives have wanted as much education for the lower classes as would make them competent workers and effective soldiers and have thought that the basics were quite enough, while liberals have wanted an education in the basics to be the first step on the road to some form of spiritual emancipation. The liberal ideal, in short, was to produce what my colleague Ben Barber has nicely baptized "an aristocracy of everyone."[9] What that means, and whether it can be achieved, is exactly what this book is about. So I should end these introductory remarks by sketching the philosophy of education that underpins what follows. It is a philosophy that could sustain a much more conservative view of education than my own, and it could doubtless sustain a much more radical view, too. Indeed, it should be said that throughout this book "liberal education" bears two distinct meanings, what one might call "*liberal* education" and "liberal-education." The former refers to the kind of education that sustains a liberal society, while the latter refers to the modern equivalent of the non-vocational education that was thought to fit a young man to behave as a "gentleman." What makes the two sorts of liberal education one subject matter is the belief that a widely disseminated liberal education in the second sense is an essential element in a liberal education in the first sense.

Existentialist philosophers have described the human condition as that of being "thrown into the world." But that is only a dramatic way of making an obvious—if important—point. We are born to parents we did not choose, and into a society we know nothing of when we arrive in it. Growing up, we acquire personalities we may or may not like; we face problems we had no part in creating; and we must use resources we do not fully understand. We must learn to deal with the environment we have been thrown into. Much that we learn, we learn for the sake of physical survival; we avoid dangerous plants, speeding trucks, and enraged parents, and discover the whereabouts of food, shelter, and employment. This is empirical knowledge. Humans can think about it more self-consciously than animals can, but it is still "basic" knowledge, and knowledge of the basics. Much of it is "picked up" rather than taught, and much of it needs no institutional teaching. It is not an accident that public education *for all* is a very recent phenomenon. The need for a working population competent in the three R's arose only in the nineteenth century, and the need for a working population competent in more than that only in the late twentieth century.

The ideas we most mind about have little to do with bare survival; and the history even of elementary public education has never been determined by questions of productivity alone. The initial impetus to basic literacy in western Europe was provided by the Protestant Reformation of the sixteenth century; when the Bible was readily available in the vernacular, and every reader was supposed to be able to work out his own salvation with its aid, reading took on a new importance. Rural communities in Scotland and the American colonies were often extremely proud of their village schools, and with good reason. Nor was it only for reasons of religious conviction that education could seem to be a public responsibility. Horace Mann wanted common schools to create Americans out of the assorted immigrants who flooded into the United States in the early nineteenth century. The British were induced to institute compulsory primary education in 1870 by the sight of

INTRODUCTION

Prussian nationalism and Prussian military prowess rather than by the needs of British industry or by Matthew Arnold's *Culture and Anarchy*. The ideas that schools inculcate when they inculcate a sense of national identity—or religious destiny, or cultural possibility—are interpretative, not barely factual. This is not to say that they have no practical impact. They affect our willingness to work, our willingness to fight, and our willingness to pay taxes to support museums and concert halls and colleges. They thus affect our society's productivity and its standing in the world; but they do it by teaching "values" and creating particular kinds of character. The rising Asian economies of the past few years have inspired questions about "Confucian capitalism"—an economic system in which citizens' loyalty to family, society, and tradition is preserved and people work, trade, and invest for essentially unselfish but nonetheless highly effective reasons. If Confucian capitalism does exist, and if it is superior to the individualistic capitalism of the West, it is not only because Japanese and Singaporean and South Korean students know more facts than Western students but because they interpret the world differently.

Education is concerned with both sorts of knowledge. They are not always easy to distinguish from each other, but at the extremes they are very different; everyday standards of truth and falsehood apply easily to technical knowledge and rather badly to elaborate interpretative theories. If the line between them is not always easy to draw, one test is the emotions they arouse. A driver's ed teacher who makes a mistake about the local speed limits is, by any view, incompetent; a social studies teacher who per-

INTRODUCTION

suades his class that the United States is *essentially* racist
is, from one political perspective, deeply wicked and, from
the opposite perspective, a liberator. A Florida school board
a few years ago demanded that local teachers should teach
their students that the American social system is "the best
in the world." The mind boggles at the folly of the school
board's supposing that teachers can so easily convey to their
students convictions that they do not feel, but more at its
inability to see the difference between simple empirical
truth and debatable moral judgment. The line between
them is blurred in sophisticated historical and literary anal-
ysis; but in the classroom the difference between education
and indoctrination is, or should be, sacred.

The view of education that underpins what follows is
this: an education that does not supply us with basic tools
for dealing with the world is no education at all. As the
world becomes economically more elaborate, these tools
change, and the content of education must change, too.
Some tools are so basic and so much a precondition of
learning anything else that they are ordinarily learned
without noticing and long before a child reaches school.
Habits of attention to what others are saying, the ability
to keep quiet and wait one's turn in discussion, courtesy
in response—all are essential to being an adept learner, and
to almost all forms of employment. We take them so much
for granted that we notice their absence as something painful and astonishing; but they are skills, habits, and knowledge that are certainly learned, and the sooner the better,
since if they are not taught early it is almost impossible to
undo the damage later. Beyond these lie what are conventionally thought of as the basics. To read and write our

native tongue fluently—enough to follow a computer manual, paraphrase the front page of *The Washington Post*, and write down directions to enable a stranger to drive from New York to, say, Oswego or Ithaca, is the first and most essential element of the basics. For a person thus armed, there is almost no form of employment that is absolutely closed, since almost any form of training then becomes imaginable.

But literacy is of little use unless complemented by numeracy. Here, too, a basic grasp is not very hard to assess. Basic numeracy includes the abilities to balance a checkbook and square the bank's statement with our own records, to understand graphs and charts in a newspaper, to give a quick answer to questions about time, mileage, gas consumption, and the like, and to know what difference it would make to use different starting and ending points for time series and different scales for bar charts.

A grasp of our national history, an acquaintance with Keats or Robert Frost, some sense of why and how Bach is different from Beethoven are not in the same sense "basic." The traditional three R's have a real priority over everything else. Certainly, a humane and rational school will teach literacy through poetry and plays, and through history and geography; if students are to learn to write clear and cogent prose, they have to start very young, and they must have something to write about—so why not the Greek myths, African folktales, the history of the foundation of whatever state of the union they happen to live in? There is no reason why mathematical facility should not be inculcated by getting students to work out how much food Sherman's army would have needed on its march from

Atlanta to Columbia. But in the narrowest sense, a child *could* be brought up to be a wholly effective philistine. Indeed, the British House of Commons and the American House of Representatives sometimes seem to be full of just such people. All the same, if a cultivated spirit is not necessary for survival, a modest sense of what our own society's cultural allegiances are is increasingly so. Which brings us to cultural literacy.

Ten years ago, E. D. Hirsch coined the wonderful phrase "cultural literacy" to describe the "vague knowledge" of our civilization that he thought we needed to function in a complicated modern society. He lumped too many different things together, but his basic insight was absolutely right. There is more to life than making a bare living and avoiding jail; to communicate with a wider range of people than our immediate friends and neighbors demands some ability to understand and empathize with the way other people interpret the world. To find our way around our own society with any degree of fluency demands more than the basics. That more is cultural literacy. This is why I have so stressed the importance of interpretative knowledge—leaving philosophical questions about the extent to which *all* knowledge is interpretative to one side as irrelevant to our purposes—and why I want to draw a sharp line between the basic competences that we would need in any modern society and what we need in particular cultural settings, our own above all. Hirsch upset some of his readers by being so ready to produce long lists of the scraps of information that the culturally literate possess. They thought he had confused the acquisition of culture with the acquisition of the skills needed to play Trivial Pursuit.

INTRODUCTION

Is knowing, roughly, who Babe Ruth was—that he played baseball rather than football, that he hit a slew of home runs, and so on and so forth—really evidence of cultured sensibilities? Of course, the answer is no. But that was not, and is not, the point.

The point is that full membership in our sort of society requires the kind of knowledge that Hirsch pointed to. Some of it is better picked up in front of the television set and on the school bus than in the classroom. A great deal of it has to come from school. It is in this category that a reasonable outline knowledge of the history of the United States comes; it is in this category that a lot of literature must come. It is not possible, and it would anyway be undesirable, for a school to persuade every one of its students that Walt Whitman's poetry was one of nineteenth-century America's greatest achievements. But it is possible for every school to ensure that all their students know "about" Whitman in the way that any fifty-year-old American knows "about" Babe Ruth. Scientific knowledge at first glance presents an obvious obstacle to this kind of understanding. Anyone who can read can read Whitman; not everyone who can read can read the Einstein-Bohr correspondence for pleasure, let alone profit. This objection misses the point Hirsch has in mind. We know about Babe Ruth without knowing how to hit home runs, and we know the skills he possessed without having to possess them ourselves. There is a form of knowledge about baseball, as there is about poetry and history, physics and chemistry, that does demand the ability to play the game, but there is a kind of knowledge that does not. To know at the crudest level how the discovery of nuclear fission and the invention of the transistor have transformed our world since 1945 is to know quite a lot about the state of our culture.

Hirsch likes an education in which we know an awful lot of different facts about the world; some of this liking is the other face of an irritation with the contempt with which influential writers such as John Dewey seemed to view "mere" facts. Dewey, of course, wanted students to acquire sound habits of inquiry, to learn how to frame hypotheses about the world, and how to discover by experiment and other forms of investigation what they needed to know. In that sense, he wanted education to go beyond the acquisition of facts. The contrast is nonetheless something of a fraud. Dewey was bored to death at school, was a ferocious enemy to rote learning, and was an advocate of an education that emphasized the *significance* of the facts children learned. No scientist has ever belittled the importance of factual information, and Dewey regarded scientific inquiry as a model for all inquiry. What is more nearly true is this: Hirsch argues for the usefulness of cultural literacy, but Dewey did not.

To see why that matters—and why even this account of the contrast is not *entirely* true—I must turn to the last step in my argument about the purpose of education. Cultural literacy is properly placed in the same category as basic literacy and basic numeracy even though it is a different kind of knowledge, because the argument for ensuring that everyone leaves school culturally literate is an argument for ensuring that everyone leaves school able to live a tolerably happy and useful life in the particular society he will enter. But there remains a difference between

INTRODUCTION

knowing about Babe Ruth and playing baseball—even badly—in order to see "from the inside" the *point* of playing like Babe Ruth. There is a difference between knowing about Walt Whitman and Robert Frost and trying to write a poem oneself, and therefore knowing from the inside what it is like to write a poem. Virginia Woolf disliked Bertrand Russell but after meeting him at dinner noted in her diary: "I should like to have the run of that headpiece." What she wanted was not to *be* Russell but to know from the inside what it was like to think as lucidly and as powerfully as Russell.

As part of liberal education, this understanding "from the inside" is valuable because it is "participatory." As an element in education, its purpose is to make us owners of the cultures we inhabit and the traditions we inherit. We want not only to know what the main events in our country's history are but to see how to write or rewrite some of the narrative ourselves. We want to know *that* Einstein unsettled the view of the universe that Newton had established, and to see *how* by being able to work through some of the triumphs of the Newtonian system for ourselves, so as to understand what crumbled and what remains intact after Einstein. We cannot explore our entire cultural inheritance; and some of it will be inaccessible to us even if we spend a lot of time exploring it, though it will not be so to others. If you are tone-deaf, you will have a harder time with music than with biology, and if you have blurred vision, you may find the art of the miniaturist a closed book. What you learn about whatever is not a closed book, however, is how to participate as a creator, not only as a spectator.

INTRODUCTION

In its American incarnation, this is a goal marked out by its strikingly democratic character. Other societies have thought of liberal education as the education of a "gentleman"—the creation of gentlemen was John Henry Newman's definition of the purpose of a university in *The Idea of a University*—and almost all societies that have thought of the question at all have thought of liberal education as something contrasted with vocational education, and therefore as something to which ordinary people would not have access. Newman, interestingly enough, did not accept the contrast; he thought that a liberal education equipped its possessors to embark on an indefinite range of careers. But even he accepted that there was a distinction between liberal education and what we now term "training." To wish everyone to have both the skills that they require to earn a living and the sense of cultural ownership that was once the prerogative of the few is certainly a new, and maybe even an impossible, ambition.

The three chapters that follow are not entirely like one another. The third is an exasperated response to the follies of the "culture wars" of the 1980s and early 1990s, when the American higher education system was the target of enraged denunciations from conservative publicists and propagandists. My view is simple enough: there is a great deal wrong with American higher education, and the elite institutions that particularly aroused the ire of the conservative critics shelter their share of human frailty. But most of the conservatives' complaints were off-target, and the effect of their noise was to divert attention from the real ills of contemporary higher education. The third lecture, therefore, begins by taking on a few of the noisier complaints of recent years and continues with more complaints of my own. I end cheerfully, however. The critics of American higher education and I share the belief that the higher reaches of the educational system often do, but should do much more often, many things that are wonderful and irreplaceable, and I end by celebrating the possibility of doing more of them for more students.

The first two chapters are different and share a common purpose of their own. That purpose is to set our contemporary educational anxieties in a larger political, cultural, and religious landscape. The pressures on education in the United States and other North Atlantic societies are part of the long process of democratization, industrialization, and secularization. The nature of the process was clear enough to many of our nineteenth-century predecessors, and they understood that it would give rise to three large problems—first, the political integration of the previously silent: the poor, the working class, and women in particular; second, the education of children who were to join an industrial workforce rather than a rural workforce, with all that implies about the problems of industrial and vocational education; and third, the preservation of "high" culture in the face of the erosion of social privilege and the erosion of the religious framework that once gave that culture its particular meaning.

My first chapter tackles this subject from the standpoint of the liberal ambition to create a society governed by what John Stuart Mill and John Dewey both called "intelligence." Just as our current anxieties about education are primarily anxieties about something else—economic inequality, social decay, technological unemployment, as I have suggested—so the nineteenth century's hopes for, and anxieties about, education were part of a much broader concern to create an entire society that could be intelligently self-governing, and not at the mercy of tradition, superstition, or whatever a harsh nature and ill-understood social change might throw at it. In this larger perspective, formal educational institutions played a subordinate role.

It is a commonplace, but still not well enough known, that colleges and universities in their modern form are very recent creations. So, too, are public high schools intended to serve the vast majority of fourteen- to eighteen-year-olds. What actually goes on in colleges and universities has an equally short history. Today, we associate a university as distinct from a college with the idea that the former will be dedicated to research. The idea that research is the major task of a university arrived in the United States only in the 1860s, and was wholeheartedly embodied in an institution only in 1876 with the foundation of The Johns Hopkins University. Most research is, of course, still done outside universities—in commercial laboratories, government research institutes, and the rest. So little is the university the only natural home of research that even much of what is done in universities is done for some other organization than the sheltering university, in the way that the Princeton Plasma Physics Laboratory, for instance, is managed by Princeton University for the federal government. In Europe, much of what is done in the "research university" sector of American higher education has always been done in institutes separate from the universities that provide mass higher education.

The orientation of the research doubtless varies, depending on whether it's done for government, for industry, or "for its own sake." Everyone who has worked in the three different environments knows that in the commercial field there is every reason *not* to publish one's results while in the "pure" field the equally savage competition is to be the *first* to publish new results. Yet everyone who works in a university laboratory also knows the pressures of looking for funding and in that sense behaving like his or her commercial colleagues. In short, just what colleges and universities are for, and which of the activities they shelter are most properly at home there, is an unsettled question— not because we have forgotten a previously agreed-upon answer but because there has never been one. Where matters seem settled, they are hardly matters of deep educational theory: in the United States, it has been decided that legal and medical training will occur at a post-graduate level in law schools and medical schools. It is essentially a professional judgment that certain undergraduate courses constitute "pre-law" and "pre-med" training. The existence of pre-law and pre-med students makes a difference to liberal arts teaching only to the degree that colleges and universities are squeamish about providing "pre-corporate" education.

Two thoughts animate chapters 2 and 3 without constituting their main topic. The first is that liberals have wanted what one might call "an educating society." In *Liberalism and Social Action*, Dewey repudiated "the planned society" that so many of his Marxist contemporaries were eager to institute in the United States as they thought it had been instituted in the Soviet Union. Certainly he was hostile to the chaotic, decayed capitalism of the Depression—but what he wished to see replace it was "the *planning* society." A planned society sounded too much like something that a God-like figure with a blueprint and a rule book had set down once and for all. A *planning* society was one that took control of its own future flexibly and open-mindedly, setting nothing in stone. By the same token, "an educated society" strikes too finished a note, as though we had done our lessons once and for all, had satisfied teacher, and were therefore educated. An *educating* society is one that tries to maximize the intelligence and perceptiveness of all its citizens, while recognizing that we do not divide naturally into teachers and taught, and that there is no curriculum laid up in a pedagogical heaven.

The second thought is that the concern with education is only artificially confined to the limits set by my subject and my focus. It was a *self-educating society* that Mill and Arnold, Emerson and Dewey were concerned with. Dewey was once asked by *The New York Times* to write an article on schools in utopia. He began, "In utopia there are no schools."[10] When Pericles made his great Funeral Oration to the Athenians—at a time when they were ravaged by plague and had suffered terrible losses in the early battles of the Peloponnesian War—his boast was, "We call ourselves the school of Hellas." Dewey meant that in an ideal world we would not have to send our children to special institutions to learn what they needed; Pericles meant that walking the Athenian streets and engaging with the Athenian citizenry could teach all Greeks what they needed to know about the good life. Every teacher who fears that students' visions of the world are shaped by the Simpsons and MTV rather than their high school classes on Shakespeare and Schubert makes Pericles' point in reverse. A *dis*-educating society is not a favorable background to the schooling process. This point has become such a cliché that I try not to belabor it too frequently hereafter; but, like other clichés, it has become a cliché because it is glaringly and obviously true, and it is well not to ignore it.

1

CULTURE AND ANXIETY

Some Autobiography

A society that embodies liberal values—that encourages economic ambition and emphasizes individual choice, that espouses the meritocratic route to social mobility and takes for granted the variability of our tastes and allegiances— may be inimical to the values embodied in traditional liberal education. There is a tension between the self-assertion that a modern liberal society fosters and the humility required of someone who tries to immerse herself in the thoughts and sentiments of another writer or another culture; there is perhaps a greater tension still between the thought that *some* achievements in philosophy, art, or literature will stand for all time and the ambition to use those achievements as stepping-stones to something better. It may be a healthy tension rather than a simple contradiction; renewing the gentlemanly ideal celebrated in Cardinal Newman's *The Idea of a University* in a liberal democracy perhaps requires us to live with such a tension. But this is something to be argued for rather than taken on trust.

I begin with a little autobiography because my own education was itself a training in how to live with this tension. I am what British observers of a certain age call a

ALAN RYAN

"scholarship boy": the beneficiary of a meritocratic educational system that plucked boys like myself (girls, too, but less often) from working-class and lower-middle-class backgrounds in order to give us what the clever children of the professional middle classes got automatically—a fiercely academic secondary education, available to London children at schools like St. Paul's, Westminster, Dulwich College, or the City of London School. I was a suitable case for treatment. My grandfathers were a miner and a truck driver; my parents left school at thirteen to work as a boy clerk and a housemaid. My father was a self-improving sort, though without the hard-driving qualities the label suggests. The family dynamo was my mother. Her fearlessness and organizational drive have been inherited by my sister, who runs one of Britain's largest community colleges, and is the only woman in such a position. In World War II, my father worked as a clerk in the Royal Artillery, and his commander was impressed enough to urge him to get professional qualifications after the war. He duly did so; my first post-1945 memories are of my father reading endless correspondence units for his accountancy examinations.

I benefited more from his efforts than he did. He became the chief financial officer of a mid-sized company and prospered, but throughout his career he preferred the company of a book to that of his fellow executives. I got the liberation he hankered after. My North London "council school"—the local public elementary school—was run by two ambitious head teachers on the lookout for clever and energetic children; they got on well with my parents, and together they set my brain in motion. Tracking—what the British call "streaming"—has become unpopular, but I en-

[44]

joyed going through school at my own speed, helped by teachers who were tough about making me get things right and imaginative about pushing me forward. The post-1945 London County Council, which ran the schools, was a model of old-fashioned social democratic virtue, but it was a liberal education that we received. We visited museums and grand houses; we sang Handel, Arne, and Purcell; and we had Benjamin Britten's *Young Person's Guide to the Orchestra* played to us by the London Symphony Orchestra under Malcolm Sargent. I was also in debt to the librarians at the local public library, who enjoyed dispensing the riches of their Aladdin's cave.

The London County Council awarded scholarships to various public schools—in the English sense of that expression—and I was awarded one to Christ's Hospital. The school had been founded in 1552 by the saintly boy king Edward VI as part of his plan for putting redundant monastic buildings scattered about London to charitable use. Christ's Hospital was meant to rescue poor but honest children, and on the whole it did. (It was one of a group of institutions of which the best known was the older foundation of Bethlehem Hospital, or Bedlam; visitors to London could watch the lunatics in their asylum and the boys of Christ's Hospital at their meals and prayers.) In 1903, the school moved into the countryside—medieval drainage and the proximity of Newgate Prison bred diphtheria— and set up near Horsham in Sussex. Entry to the school was "means-tested": if your parents could afford to pay for a private education, you couldn't go. My family couldn't afford to pay for my education, so I went. Americans with children at private colleges and universities will be familiar with financial aid given on this basis; in Britain it still remains an oddity.

During the 1950s, Christ's Hospital was as meritocratic as my elementary school had been in the late 1940s. Most boys left at sixteen to join the sort of City of London firm that had for two centuries employed them in clerical jobs. Charles Lamb was the most famous of them; he spent his working life in the East India Company and his evenings writing the *Essays of Elia* and drinking tea with William Godwin. The small number who could tackle academic disciplines to a level that would get them into Oxford and Cambridge stayed on till eighteen; they included Samuel Taylor Coleridge. The purest example of the self-made academic that the school produced was Sir Henry Maine, the great nineteenth-century jurist and legal historian and a man with a lifelong hunger for academic glory and financial security. I am less driven than he, but I know that I have spent my life trying to meet the standards set for me at Christ's Hospital.

I am vain enough to think the raw material my teachers worked with must have been good enough to inspire such efforts on their part, but my chief sensation is astonishment at my luck at falling in with the people who taught me in Islington, Horsham, and Oxford. For an anxious lower-middle-class child, conscious of the tight budgeting that went on at home and the sacrifice of the present to the future that defines English middle-class life, it was an unspeakable luxury to find this rich and vivid world to which the price of admission was only the desire to join. My brave new world was peopled with writers and my Ellis Island was the school library. There is almost no platitude about the pleasure of having your eyes opened and your mind stretched to which I do not subscribe. At its best, liberal education opens a conversation between ourselves and the immortal dead, gives us voices at our shoulders asking us to think again and try harder—sometimes by asking us *not* to think but just to look and listen, to try *less* hard, and to wait for the light to dawn. It is not always at its best, and the contrast between what *can* happen and what more commonly does is not to be blinked at. Even when liberal education is not at its best, however, it is well worth defending against its wilder critics.

Meritocracy, For and Against

I was not special; innumerable students have had the experience I had; and innumerable students still get the care I got. I mention my education to make a general point about the idea of meritocracy and the pursuit of excellence. Liberalism has a natural affinity with meritocracy; it is attracted to an aristocracy of talent and critical of an aristocracy of birth. Liberal education in the conventional sense also rests on the thought that an acquaintance with intellectual, literary, and artistic excellence is in some (rather debatable and hotly debated) fashion good for us, and that one of the ways it is so is in teaching us to measure ourselves against touchstones of cultural and intellectual excellence. My reflexes are meritocratic. Let me take an embarrassing example. *The Bell Curve*'s claim that measured differences in IQ between black and white Americans reflect different "racial" endowments of native intelligence is entirely ill-founded, and the insinuating tone of the book unpleasant.[1] Its insistence that people should be selected for jobs, graduate training, university admission, and the like on the basis of measurable competence is, however, impossible to resist. The cliché defense of meritocracy is that none of us wants to be operated on by an incompetent brain surgeon. That suggests a rather narrow idea of merit; the principle applies more widely. Nobody wants Pushkin translated by someone who knows no Russian, nor do we want the Cleveland Orchestra conducted by a tone-deaf lout with no sense of rhythm. The fact that we can debate the merits of different translations of Pushkin and different performances of *The Rite of Spring* while conceding that all are technically competent makes no difference. Where there is a measurable skill, it should be measured, and the excellent should be preferred to the merely decent. Where standards are debatable, they should be debated. The point is well understood by sports fans, but underappreciated in the arts and humanities.

The case for meritocracy is so obvious that it is tempting to forget that there are respectable arguments against it.[2] Some have been prominent in American life. Let me mention two. First, what we seek in most areas of life is not "the best" but "the good-enough." And rightly so. The restless search for the excellent automobile that an automotive perfectionist engages in does not increase his driving pleasure; it merely deprives him of the enjoyment that he would have had if he had settled for a merely decent car. Applied to education, the thought is that most students in high school and college will learn *enough* math and *enough* writing and reading skills to get a decent living. They need not be made anxious and dissatisfied by having to face the fact that they will never be very good in either field. Nor is there much of an economic argument for pursuing intellectual excellence. The economy needs very few excellent mathematicians, but a lot of averagely numerate workers. There is an economic case for insisting on a competitive marketplace and the development of excellent products and excellent management, but not for insisting on meritocracy—as distinct from competence—in the educational sphere. Experience suggests that this is a sound view: the United States is the most productive country in the world; its popular culture is as attractive to other countries as its technical expertise in aeronautical engineering and computer software. It is neither an intellectually rigorous nor a culturally ambitious society, however; outside major metropolitan areas, there are few bookshops, the radio plays an unending diet of gospel or country and western music, and intellectual pretensions are not encouraged. The nation has prospered without inculcating in its young people the cultural and intellectual ambitions that French lycées and German gymnasia inculcate in their students. Why should it change now?

Most Americans are happy to compete in the marketplace on the basis of the excellence of their products, but few wish to be more discriminating, better read, or whatever else, than their neighbors. Most people regard what appears to be intellectual discussion rather as a way of cementing friendly relations among themselves than as a way of changing minds or seeking truth. Many conservatives in the 1990s have looked back nostalgically to the 1950s. But in the 1950s American high schools taught "Life Adjustment" classes. Among the topics covered in one New York

State school system described by Richard Hofstadter in *Anti-intellectualism in American Life* were "Developing School Spirit," "My Duties as a Baby-Sitter," "Clicking with the Crowd," "What Can Be Done about Acne?" "Learning to Care for My Bedroom," "Making My Room More Attractive." Eighth-grade pupils were given these questions on a true-false test: "Just girls need to use deodorants"; "Cake soap can be used for shampooing." Women friends of mine were taught how to enter and leave a sports car without allowing their skirts to ride up and expose their underwear. If the 1950s were wonderful, it is not because they were years of universal intellectual excellence.[3]

A second persuasive objection to meritocracy rests on a related but rather different thought: most people prefer stability, authority, and tradition to uncertainty, free thinking, and openness to the future. Where merit is clearly defined and relevant, persons should be promoted, and ideas accepted, on their merits; otherwise, habits of acceptance should be cherished. This is an old conservative thought, and it is very hard to resist. Karl Popper, the philosopher of science, social theorist, and author of *The Open Society and Its Enemies*, defended the idea that the policies of governments, like scientific theories, and social practices generally, should be accepted strictly on their merits, precisely because he thought that the "normal" condition of mankind was conservative and, indeed in his eyes, "tribal." This was why the "open society"—a liberal, democratic, changeable, and argumentative society—had so many enemies, from the high-minded philosopher Plato at one extreme to low-minded terrorists such as Hitler and Stalin at the other. Popper's model of the open society was a community of research scientists. Science is a strikingly artificial activity: scientists have to formulate bold hypotheses about how the world works and then submit these hypotheses to rigorous testing against whatever evidence can be found. Hypotheses may not be protected from refutation by appealing to our own virtues and our critics' vices, or indeed by appealing to anything but the best available evidence. If *The Bell Curve*'s hypothesis that IQ is racially determined is to be tested scientifically, we must not try to discredit it by observing that one of its authors was a Jew who naturally liked the idea that science showed that Jews were innately more clever than blacks; and it won't do to defend it by observing that many of its most savage critics were blacks who naturally disliked the same idea.

Conservatives are sometimes criticized for advocating laissez-faire in economics but wanting stability in religious, social, and cultural matters. This seems a mistake; it may not be possible to have what they want, but the combination of stability in our deepest allegiances and quick-footedness in our habits of work and consumption would surely make for a happy and prosperous society. A greater source of anxiety today is that it is not groups who *enjoy* the pace of change in American economic and social life who want stability in their deepest beliefs. Recently, the threat to free speech and free inquiry on American campuses has come—as it has done for most of the century —not from the defenders of private property or the defenders of upper-class respectability but from lower-middle-class groups demanding "respect" for themselves, their opinions, and their culture. The latter are not defending privileges that have come under attack but seeking comfort in a world they view as hostile and dangerous. Fundamentalist Christians—almost invariably from rather humble backgrounds—who try to stop colleges and universities preaching tolerance for the sexual tastes of gays and lesbians genuinely feel as ill-used as the gays and lesbians who want their schools to protect them against the insults of the godly.

The liberal view is hostile to the search for comfort and support, at least partly for meritocratic reasons. All sides are entitled to physical safety, and certainly everyone needs friends, but nobody is entitled to *respect*—other than the minimal respect that is involved in arguing courteously with one's opponents rather than beating them up. Or, rather, one is entitled to be treated as a rational adult, but one's ideas are entitled only to the respect they earn by being properly thought out, factually well grounded, and the like. It is this distinction that many students, particularly students from families with no previous experience of academic life, find it hard to deal with. The thought that much of what they have hitherto unhesitatingly believed is false, misguided, or simply one among many options produces a lot of anxiety. The wish to assuage this anxiety runs headlong into the view that we must try to believe only those ideas that are good enough to stand up to criticism. None of this licenses rudeness or brutality; it is no doubt true that many professors are socially inept, and others are authoritarian, and still others are so insecure that they cannot bear any criticism of their opinions. All the same, even if we were all as deft and sensitive as could be imagined, the ideal classroom would not be a cozy place.

CULTURE AND ANXIETY

Part of the object of education is to teach us to treat our own ideas objectively rather than subjectively; we ought not to want to believe what won't stand up to criticism, though we all do, and we can hardly hope to discover which of our beliefs are more and which less reliable without a few moments of discomfort. Bullying and insult are intolerable, no matter who is on the receiving end; but shading the truth is the ultimate academic sin.

Liberal Anxieties and Conservative Anger

My first insights into my own education came through reading John Stuart Mill's *Autobiography* and progressing from Matthew Arnold's "Scholar Gypsy" to grappling with Lionel Trilling's *Matthew Arnold*. A predictable result of a liberal education is that its beneficiaries behave like the hero of Saul Bellow's novel *Herzog*—who spent much of his time composing postcards to the immortal dead. Writing about education is particularly likely to involve such a one-way traffic in postcards. Jaroslav Pelikan recently wrote *The Idea of a University: A Reexamination* to defend a conservative and traditionalist vision of higher education in homage to and in dialogue with Cardinal Newman. My antipathy to organized religion, to the Oxford movement, and to the personality of Newman himself means that I admire Newman's prose without much liking the writer. Moreover, Newman wrote *The Idea of a University* to defend the newly founded University College, Dublin, against fellow Catholics who wished it to provide a sectarian education; and this is hardly our situation. We are more likely either to ignore the education of all but an elite or else to be besotted by the needs of the economy. My own touchstone is a book that nobody wrote—*Culture and Anxiety*[4]—but the voices in my head are those of Mill, Arnold, Russell, and Dewey, and, among recent writers, Raymond Williams and Richard Hoggart. Since they were considerable readers, I therefore eavesdrop on their conversations with Marx, Hegel, Freud, Carlyle, and innumerable others.

Liberalism has for two hundred years suffered from three great anxieties. The first is fear of the culturally estranged condition of what has been variously called the "underclass," the "unwashed mob," the *lumpenproletariat*, or (by Hegel) the *Pöbel*; the second is unease about "disenchantment," the loss of a belief that the world possesses a religious and spiritual meaning; the third is fear that the degeneration of the French Revolution between 1789 and 1794 into a regime of pure terrorism was only the harbinger of revolutions to come. These fears often feed on one another. "We must educate our masters," said the English politician Sir Robert Lowe when he saw that he could no longer resist the Reform Bill of 1867. That legislation gave the vote to most of the adult male inhabitants of Britain's cities. Lowe was frightened by a familiar scenario: unless the working class was educated, farsighted, and prudent, commercial and industrial change would bring in its wake a democratic revolution which would degenerate into mob rule and end with a guillotine in Hyde Park. In the alternative, there would be no revolution, because the mob would follow the first golden-tongued demagogue who cared to woo them. Arnold feared the mob. Mill did not, but he feared Napoléon III. Their contemporary, social theorist Alexis de Tocqueville, gave Europeans some understanding of how the Americans had escaped both of these disastrous sequences while the French had not.

These political fears are today antiquated in Britain and the United States—but Britain and the United States remain unusual. The recent civil wars in the former Communist state of Yugoslavia are but one of many contemporary instances of the way political and economic disruption leads to irrational, violent, and atavistic behavior. They seem to indicate that the first thing a newly emancipated and politically uneducated people will do is follow a dictator. Franjo Tudjman and Slobodan Milosevic are nastier and more uncouth than Napoléon III; but everyone who saw Louis-Bonaparte, the nephew of Napoléon and an adventurer of the lowest kind, rise to power after the French Revolution of 1848, *on the back of the popular vote*, knew how a demagogue could turn the popular vote into a mandate for his dictatorial ambitions.

I want to emphasize the difference between these fears, however. It is clear that we might escape the guillotine but relapse into mindlessness; we might lead culturally vivid lives under the shadow of the guillotine; we might escape both these fates but feel intolerably estranged from the world because a life without strong religious sentiments turns out to be humanly impossible. The three great anxieties are different: the first rests on the idea of a distinctively *cultural* disaster, what Arnold termed "the *brutalisation* of the masses"; the second rests on the idea that if religious faith and a sense of community together decay, we shall be "unanchored" in the world; the third is more narrowly the fear of political violence. Nineteenth-century Britain and the United States—where modern liberal education was invented—suffered these anxieties to different degrees and in different forms. The French Revolution did not haunt the American political imagination as it haunted British and European writers; indeed, only with the rediscovery of Edmund Burke's attacks on the French Revolution by American conservatives such as Russell Kirk and William F. Buckley during the Cold War did the political excesses of the French Revolution become a theme for American political controversy. Conversely, fear of the solvent effect of immigration affected nineteenth-century Britain only in the narrow and highly specific form of a dislike for Irish migrants in the 1840s and for Jewish and other Eastern European migrants in the last two decades of the century; but in the United States the fear that immigrants from anywhere other than England, Scotland, or Protestant Northern Europe would erode the existing common culture was one source of the demand for "common schools" as early as the 1830s, and variations on that theme have been heard in American politics ever since.

I call these anxieties "liberal anxieties," but an obvious objection is that they are *everyone's* anxieties. My response is that both *anxiety* and *liberal* are to be taken seriously. Liberals have always been on the side of economic, political, and intellectual change; they have hoped that change would culminate in freedom rather than chaos or estrangement, but they have always known that they might unleash forces they could not control. The late eighteenth-century conservative and bitter enemy of the French Revolution, Joseph de Maistre, denounced the liberal philosophers of the eighteenth century for encouraging the aspirations of the common people, and so inciting revolution and bloodshed.

CULTURE AND ANXIETY

As he observed, it is not the tiger we blame for rending its victim but the man who lets him off the leash. Liberals have wished to raise expectations without being overwhelmed by the consequences, and it is none too clear that it can be done. Tocqueville famously argued that the French Revolution broke out because the population had made enough progress in the years before 1789 to be maddened when progress was not sustained. Americans commenting on the fact that black Americans were more aggressive in demanding their rights *after* Jim Crow legislation had been overturned always refer to what Adlai Stevenson described as "a revolution of rising expectations." It is all too plausible that people who have never been able to raise their eyes to new possibilities will remain docile, while those who have seen new possibilities will rebel if they are then denied the chance to seize them. Liberal anxiety responds to the risk of such a revolution.

Liberals know that it is not irrational to bet against the liberal project from the right or the left, or from both sides at once—that it is quite rational to think that change should be approached much more cautiously, or that it must be embraced much more wholeheartedly. In intellectual and cultural matters, indeed, liberals themselves are often conservative and revolutionary simultaneously in just this way. They see that they are the inheritors of traditions they do not themselves wish to overthrow, but they want everyone to explore those traditions for themselves. When they do so, they may reject them or alter them out of all recognition. The liberal can only respond that this tension lies at the heart of all serious intellectual or aesthetic activity. How could a scientist proceed if not by absorbing the techniques and theories and problems of a tradition of inquiry and then launching out into new work; and are not scientists often disconcerted to find their cherished ideas dismissed as old hat by their radical juniors? Is not the same thing true in art and music?

The concepts of "conservative," "liberal," and "revolutionary" in intellectual matters are used loosely, of course. The context in which they are used more exactly, and where liberals are habitually beset from left and right, is the political. And here is where the difference between anxiety, fear, and anger is most plainly visible. Conservatives have rightly felt *fear* in the face of the changes the liberals wanted; but since they wanted to preserve an *ancien régime* society, creedally based political authority, and the habits of a rural economy, they had no reason to be anxious but much reason to be frightened and angry. Socialists and radicals have rightly felt *exasperation* and *anger* at the inadequacy of the changes that liberals have welcomed, and at the evils liberals have left untouched as well as at the new forms of exploitation they have brought with them. Conservatives have disliked the liberal, meritocratic ideal of "the career open to talent" because they wished to preserve a society in which hereditary privilege ruled, and not always because it was in their self-interest; socialists have disliked the liberal, meritocratic ideal because it placed unskilled workers at the mercy of financially or intellectually better endowed people. Conservatives and socialists have often held in common the belief that stable societies in which people know what to expect of life are happier societies than the shifting, insecure societies that liberalism creates.

CULTURE AND ANXIETY

Nineteenth-century liberals added to their insecurity when they insisted that reform must come through the efforts of its beneficiaries. A chapter entitled "The Probable Futurity of the Labouring Classes" in Mill's *Principles of Political Economy* (1848) set out the argument. Mill took it for granted that benevolent conservatives existed; their flaw was that they wanted to look after the working class. The liberal aim was that the workers should look after themselves; the ultimate aim was a wholly classless society, where individual success depended upon merit. Mill's characteristically sharp way of putting the point was to insist that he wished to live in a society "with none but a working class." Other than children and retired people, nobody was to benefit without contributing to the best of his ability. Self-advancement required intelligence and foresight. It demanded control over fertility. It demanded equality between the sexes. It demanded a transformation of relations at work. Mill was certain—wrongly, as it turned out—that educated people would not accept forever a division between managers and workers, or between capitalists and wage earners. The title of political scientist Benjamin Barber's recent book, *An Aristocracy of Everyone*, summarizes Mill's aspirations: everyone was to make the best of herself. The revolutionary route to such a result was needlessly painful and unlikely to work; education in a broad sense was the only route. When I say education in a broad sense, I mean that Mill wanted to make society and politics generally more intelligent. He rightly had no thought of throwing open an unreformed Oxford and Cambridge to the English working class of the 1840s.

ALAN RYAN

The Idea of an Educating Society

What Mill, like Arnold, and like Emerson on the other side of the Atlantic for that matter, had in mind was the transformation of the entire society into a community that was reflective and broadly cultivated, as well as liberally educated in the usual sense. This is why I said earlier that the ideal of an educat*ing* society, rather than an educat*ed* society, was so important, and why it was the entire society rather than what we nowadays call educational institutions on which discussion focused. What role there was for the ancient English universities in such a vision was not obvious. Until they were reformed by Act of Parliament in the 1850s, they could hardly play any role. In the early nineteenth century, they were actually less open to the lower-middle-class or working-class young man than they had been three centuries earlier. What animated reformers was the hope that a more rational society would be governed by a meritocracy; once power was gained by administrative ability and professional expertise rather than by birth, it would both induce the sons of the upper classes to get a decent education, and open social and political advancement to their social inferiors. Only when major social institutions gave the stamp of approval to education would ambitious persons seek a decent education. Mill helped to govern India from the London offices of the East India Company. The company had set up a school for boys who would go out to govern India—Haileybury College —and there they got a notably modern education, including courses in economics, history, and literature of a kind that Oxford and Cambridge introduced later and reluctantly. The new colleges—such as University College, London, founded in 1828—that were founded in London and the larger provincial cities could more easily than the ancient universities dispense an education both practical and liberal throughout the population.

The wish to be able to boast of the United States or of Britain, as Pericles did of ancient Athens, that our society is a school for all the world is and always has been a utopian ambition. Moreover, it is not an ambition that we can expect everyone to see the point of. The kind of society that sets store by being as self-critical and intellectually ambitious as the society Mill hoped for will not appeal to everyone. Tastes vary. Still, it is easy to imagine that its ideals can readily be realized on a small scale in particular contexts—that liberal arts colleges will form very "Millian" communities, as will many laboratories, some firms, and even some sports teams—and that in many contexts they will not be realized at all. The improvement in working class well-being in the past hundred and fifty years has moved us both toward and away from that utopian goal. Especially in the United States, the growth of working-class incomes has produced a population that is infinitely less brutal, drunken, ignorant, and alienated than was the urban proletariat of Victorian England, let alone the denizens of New York's Hell's Kitchen seventy-five years ago. It is also a population that is emphatically private in its concerns, and in that way quite different from what Mill and even Arnold would have hoped. Only a bare majority of possible voters now go to the polls in the United States, even in presidential elections. Barely 10 percent of citizens can name their local congressman.

It would be wrong to call the citizens of the present-day United States passive or apathetic; but their concerns are domestic, private, and familial. In 1834 Tocqueville saw this retreat into domesticity as one possible American future, and it was one that he and Mill feared. A prosperous but narrowly self-centered society is better than a poor and narrowly self-centered society; but it is not what they wanted. They hoped that education would produce the wish and the ability dramatically to rebuild social, economic, and political institutions. That economic progress would remove the desire for violent revolution, by subverting the ambition for anything other than our own private well-being, would have seemed a sad bargain. If liberals have less reason than they once had to wonder whether change would not degenerate into mere chaos, they have every reason to wonder whether they were right to think that a free and prosperous society would also be lively, intelligent, and self-improving.

Brutalization

The fear of brutalization took, and still takes, different forms in Britain and America. Arnold's talk of the brutalization of the *masses* made perfect sense in a class-divided society; culture was a middle- and upper-class possession. British migrants to colonial America, on the other hand, could more plausibly fear the brutalization of a whole society in a bleak and hostile environment. What led the spiritual leaders of the Massachusetts colony to establish Harvard College in 1636 had no direct contemporary British counterpart: the feeling of being a small island of Chris-

tian culture in a vast wilderness was a *physical* reality in
the New World in a way it could not be in Britain. The
feeling was reinforced by the incessant expansion of the
country. To establish a college or university—after a
church and perhaps a local elementary school—became an
outward and visible sign of an intention to cultivate the
territory and civilize the citizenry. The process received a
great impetus when the American Revolution removed the
imperial government's constraints on expansion; but it had
already received almost as much from the revivals that were
a feature of American religious life from the early eighteenth century onwards.

Harvard was two hundred years old in 1836, and the
University of Michigan already nineteen. The College of
William and Mary was founded in 1693, but when the
elderly Jefferson founded the University of Virginia in
1819, he said it was the proudest achievement of his career.
Small liberal arts colleges proliferated in the northeastern
United States, beginning with Williams College in 1791.
The town of Evanston is today a northern suburb of Chicago, but Northwestern University is a reminder that almost the first thing that devout Methodists in the
Northwest Territory did was to build a college, just as
Oberlin College speaks to the memory of the German educator after whom it was named on its foundation in 1819.
After a church and a school, it seemed sometimes that almost the next thing that a respectable town required was
its own college; most were evanescent foundations, but
some flourished, to our great good fortune.

The cultural environments of Britain and America were
less strikingly different than the physical environments.

The frontier wilderness was hardly less propitious a setting for high culture than the spiritual wilderness of the British industrial cities in the mid-nineteenth century that so distressed Arnold and many others. Certainly, the British city called out the same response as the American frontier: local worthies and local clergy created civic colleges that eventually turned into the Universities of Manchester, or Bristol, or Leeds. Two differences have always been very marked. The first is the place of established religion and the second the place of acknowledged class distinctions. The absence of both made the United States the more plausible setting for a democratic intellectual culture; whether they also made the United States a less favorable environment for "high" culture has been argued over for a hundred and fifty years.

The United States was, and Britain was not, committed to the separation of church and state. The U.S. Constitution forbade, while the British continued to accept, hereditary titles of nobility. The fate of England's two ancient universities was tied to the fortunes of the Church of England and to the most conservative forces in national politics. In colonial and independent America alike, a student might well choose a college on the basis of religious affiliation, but there was no question of his being excluded altogether for religious reasons. Nondenominational state universities sprang up immediately after the revolution. Their presidents had often been admitted to the ministry, and a generalized piety was expected of them; but the contrast with England was striking. There the two great ancient universities were an Anglican monopoly: nobody could even begin an education at Oxford without swearing allegiance to the Church of England, while nobody could graduate from Cambridge without doing so. In both countries, of course, only a tiny percentage of the population attended college at all: Princeton graduated eight or a dozen students a year for many years after its foundation in 1746, for instance, and in Britain, Oxford was a smaller university for the two centuries after the Civil War of 1641–49 than it had been for the century before the war. The role of colleges in defeating brutalization was understood to be a matter of "trickle-down," whereby the college-educated would diffuse enlightenment either directly, through the ministry and in teaching, or indirectly, through their support of the arts, libraries, museums, and the like.

The Anglican monopoly of access to the ancient English universities was part of the Anglican monopoly of access to the learned professions, Parliament, and political preferment. Dissenters established very small colleges to train their ministers, and to provide a serious liberal education to their children. It was these dissenting colleges that eighteenth-century American colleges resembled in their seriousness, their accessibility to the relatively humble, their liveliness, and therefore their democratic potential. Indeed, when Princeton was founded in 1746, it was to the English dissenting colleges that it looked for curricular inspiration. The established English universities were very far from natural breeding grounds for a democratic culture, and in their eighteenth-century torpor were hardly an educational model of any kind. From the 1820s onwards, things changed. With the creation in 1828 of what became University College, London—"the godless college in Gower Street"—England acquired her first secular college.

ALAN RYAN

King's College, London, was founded shortly after to ensure that the capital possessed an Anglican college. Outside London, a range of colleges, often founded by Dissenters, started to reach beyond their original, sectarian clientele. The Scots, it has to be said, looked on in some amusement, having enjoyed the benefit of accessible nonsectarian universities in Edinburgh, Glasgow, and Aberdeen for several centuries. It was no wonder that *The Edinburgh Review* took particular pleasure in tweaking the noses of Oxford conservatives.

The early nineteenth century gave the critics of brutalization plenty to fear. The horrors of newly urbanizing Britain were recited by every spectator. Mill was jailed for a day at the age of sixteen for distributing birth control pamphlets to the working-class houses of the East End; it is said he did so after coming across the corpse of an abandoned baby as he walked to work at East India Company headquarters. The starved and stunted condition of the children who worked in the cotton industry was a commonplace; so was the drunken and brutal behavior of their parents; so was their almost complete alienation from the church; so were their ignorance and illiteracy. Karl Marx, who relied on Friedrich Engels's *The Condition of the Working Class in England*; Thomas Carlyle, on whose *Past and Present* Engels had himself relied a good deal; and both Mill and his father were in substantial agreement about the horrors of the situation. They were also substantially agreed that the better-off had neglected the spiritual and physical welfare of the worse-off. Revolutionary socialists such as Marx insisted that nothing would change until the expropriators were expropriated; conservative reformers such as the English humanitarian Lord Shaftesbury insisted that it was the proper task of a conservative ruling class to make coal owners and manufacturers treat their workers decently, to protect women and children from exploitation, and to secure the conditions of their spiritual growth. Paradoxically enough, it was the reports of the Factory Inspectorate that Shaftesbury and his allies had shamed the British government into establishing in 1833 on which Marx later relied when he was writing *Das Kapital*.

Disenchantment

The phenomenon of brutalization at its crudest is today a phenomenon only of the decayed inner cities of the United States and Britain. So far from proletarianization being the lot of the working class, the work and consumption habits of what used to be called the "respectable" working class have become universal. But the end of the twentieth century sees no diminution of anxiety about secularization and disenchantment. The fear has one source, but two distinct aspects. The one source is the increasingly dominant position of the physical sciences among the many ways in which we explain and understand the world. The two distinct aspects are, first, that scientific understanding will drive all the poetry out of the world—that color, beauty, sublimity will vanish, and nothing will be left but matter in motion—and, second, that in the absence of transcendental sanctions, mankind will become as the beasts, without shame, without morality, and without ambitions for perfection. The common thread is the fear that what science reveals is that human existence is accidental; the world has no purpose, humans have no special place in the world, whatever they contrive by way of an existence is wholly up to them, and in the absence of a divine ordering of the world, what they may get up to hardly bears thinking about. "If God is dead, everything is permitted," wrote Friedrich Nietzsche. Many observers of the horrors of the twentieth century have thought that the Nazi death camps were a commentary on that claim.

The Enlightenment was an amorphous movement. Not all skeptical, secular philosophers of the eighteenth century thought they belonged to the movement. Nonetheless, by the end of the eighteenth century the ideas that mankind was morally and intellectually self-sufficient, and that the world was not intrinsically mysterious but would yield to scientific investigation and control, were understood as the central ideas of the Enlightenment. The great German philosopher Immanuel Kant said that the motto of the Enlightenment was *sapere aude*, or "dare to understand." Critics of the Enlightenment complained that their enlightened opponents were bent on driving the poetry from the world, that the world described by science was cold and colorless. William Blake thought that the arrival of Newton had been the death of the human world.

This is not to say that science is irreligious. When the sociologist Max Weber introduced the idea of "disenchantment" in *The Protestant Ethic and the Spirit of Capitalism*,[5] he argued that modern science was a product of the same spiritual impulse as Protestantism. The German word usually translated as "disenchanted" is *entzaubert*, or "unmagicked." The Protestant distaste for magic was a moral and spiritual distaste. To believe in magic was an insult to

God. A serious God would not interfere with His creation in a capricious fashion; He could not be cajoled, bribed, or seduced into doing His worshipers a good turn. The Protestant God was "deus absconditus," the God who had created a universe governed by intelligible natural laws, and who had then allowed that universe to operate according to those laws. He Himself was absent. This absence left the world to be explained by whatever theories the new natural sciences could validate. This austere picture of the universe sustained, and was sustained by, an ideal of self-discipline that repudiated the use of anything other than our own talents and energy to achieve our ends. It bred a decided moral and intellectual toughness in the process.

The "enchanted" world, in contrast, was a world where we were at home. It was not necessarily a world created by, or ruled by, any of the gods of the great world religions; but it was a world where "natural piety" made sense. William Wordsworth's poetry conveys perhaps more acutely than any philosophical explanation what it was whose loss the critics of the Enlightenment lamented. The Romantic poets had no doubt that what we first encounter is an enchanted world. The child who comes into this world "trailing clouds of glory" needed no teaching or prompting to rejoice in the rainbow, or to tremble as the shadow of the mountain stole across the lake. The natural world spoke to him and he needed only to listen to it. Only when these natural reactions had been suppressed could he think that science could tell him all there is to know about the world. But the suppression of these reactions was a moral and emotional disaster, well captured in the line "shades of the prison house close around the growing boy."

ALAN RYAN

One of Matthew Arnold's more famous essays, "Science and Literature," is devoted to praising poetry and disparaging science as the basis of a concern for culture. It was written as a response to Darwin's ally, Thomas Henry Huxley, who had himself been provoked by Arnold's *Culture and Anarchy* to write in defense of science as the basis for a liberal education. The quarrel of science with poetry is a running theme in the nineteenth century, and one taken up in an interesting way by John Dewey in the twentieth. Its impact on the liberal theory of education is plain enough. Education is notoriously a solvent of traditional forms of religious belief. It is also likely to promote the belief that what cannot be explained by some kind of scientific explanation cannot be explained at all. That in turn is likely to promote a view of poetry—and with it, religion—that denies it any cognitive content, and sees it as pure self-expression, a matter of sentiment, not intellect. The thought that poetry is "only" expressive is simply the other face of the view that a strictly scientific understanding of the world is all the *understanding* that there can be. The fear, then, is that neither the individual nor society can sustain an adequate life without an individual or collective conviction that the world itself is in harmony with our desires and affections. It is the fear that we will find life thin, shallow, and unsatisfying if our individual hopes and fears are not supported by rituals, festivals, by what, if backed by a supernatural faith, we would call religious belief, and otherwise might call social poetry.

It is no accident that Arnold looked to poetry to supply what the declining credibility of Christian mythology could not, nor that Mill argued that the religion of humanity could satisfy the needs of the heart while it also reinforced the dictates of rational altruism. Once more, it is the liberal who will experience the suspicion that these palliatives may not anchor us in our world as *anxiety*; the truly devout unfeignedly believe that the visible world reposes upon something deeper; skeptical conservatives hope people won't ask whether it does. Liberals suffer a self-inflicted wound: they want the emancipation that leads to disenchantment, but want the process that emancipates us to relocate us in the world as well. Nietzsche and Weber are only the most eloquent among the voices that say it cannot be done in the way the liberal wants. The anything but eloquent Dewey is the most philosophically astute of those who say that it can.

The Terror

The terror induced by the Terror is an oft-told tale. It is not wholly true that the argument between Edmund Burke's *Reflections on the Revolution in France* and Tom Paine's *Rights of Man* ended in a knockout victory for Burke, but it is certainly true that Burke's forecast—made in 1790—of the subsequent course of the revolution was unnervingly accurate. The revolution did degenerate into terrorism, dictatorship, and ultimately the arrival of a military government. The fear that opening the gate to popular aspirations would lead inexorably to mob rule, violence, and military dictatorship, together with the ruin of the traditional aristocracy, the spoliation of the established church, and an indefinite continental war thereafter, was enough to make anyone flinch from reform. The liberal reply was naturally that the disaster occurred because reform had come too little and too late, and because good sense had been swamped by ideology. This was what Burke himself said in calmer moments; a society without the means of reform is without the means of its own preservation. The argument rattled back and forth for half a century. The young James Mill edited the *Anti-Jacobin Review* when he first came to London in 1803, but twenty years later defended the democratization of British politics in terms that led Thomas Macaulay to prophesy that if James Mill had his way, some future visitor from New Zealand would be left to stare at the ruins of St. Paul's and wonder what had happened to the British.

Macaulay was a Whig, not a Tory. As with the other anxieties of nineteenth-century liberals, left and right found matters simpler than the liberals did. Macaulay wanted to reform Parliament so that the respectable middle class could play a more active role in British politics; but he feared to go further. The Duke of Wellington and his fellow Tories thought it inconceivable that any change to so perfect a political system could be an improvement, while the Chartists wanted the demands of the People's Charter: annual elections, universal suffrage, and the secret ballot at once. Liberals remained divided among themselves, as they have been ever since. At the time of the fairly mild rioting that preceded the passing of the 1867 Reform Act, John Stuart Mill told the rioters that they should resort to insurrection only if they thought it was absolutely necessary *and* they were likely to succeed, while Matthew Arnold angrily observed: "As for rioting the Roman way was the right one; flog the perpetrators and fling the ringleaders from the Tarpeian rock."

Although Britain and the United States have possessed eminently stable political systems for many years, such arguments persist. In the 1960s, the generally liberal professors of the United States found themselves faced with student insurrection, and reacted with similar ambivalence. As young people who were at risk of being sent off to Vietnam to fight a war they disapproved of made common cause with assorted Maoists, Trotskyites, and even the Deweyan enthusiasts for industrial democracy who had created the Students for a Democratic Society, the old drama repeated itself. Badly needed reforms in teaching and administration threatened to lead to anarchy; and once the Black Panther movement joined the struggle, real violence was never further away than one twitch of a trigger finger. But whatever else was on the agenda, popular insurrection was not. What the state's role in education should be, what degree of abstention from political involvement should be practiced by universities and their faculties, what the place of formal higher education was in the promotion of high culture, and what degree of openness to "low" culture and its fads was proper to a university—these have been perennial questions. That an alliance of students and workers should form a revolutionary vanguard was at most a passing fancy of Herbert Marcuse.

Politics, Culture, Education

If these are the anxieties that beset liberals, and their connection with education is now made out—essentially, that it is not only a little learning that is a dangerous thing for social and individual stability and security—it remains to ask what the role of liberal education is in the liberal view of the world. The answer is that there is no one answer. Once that is acknowledged, it becomes clearer that many of the arguments about the expansion of college and university education over the past century have been arguments about the relative weight to be attached to the provision of a liberal education versus research on the one hand and vocational education on the other, while others have been arguments about the content of what everyone agrees to be a liberal education—what in an American university would lead to a bachelor's degree in the college of arts and sciences. A little history may be illuminating as a preface to two famous nineteenth-century arguments, whose echoes rumble on. Before the American Revolution, there were nine colleges: Harvard, founded in 1636, whose doors opened in 1638; William and Mary (1693); Yale (1701); the College of Philadelphia, later the University of Pennsylvania (1740); Princeton (1746); King's College, subsequently Columbia (1754); the College of Rhode Island, later Brown University (1764); Queen's College, later Rutgers (1766); and Dartmouth (1769). All had a common purpose, which was well expressed in the words of Princeton's founders: "Though our great intention was to found a seminary for educating ministers of the gospel, yet we hope it will be a means of raising up men that will be useful in other learned professions—ornaments of the state as well as the church."

The sharp modern distinction between "public" and "private" universities and colleges was unknown until

1819. Most colleges would have been hard-pressed to survive their early years without assistance from their state governments. But when the state of New Hampshire set out to take over the direction of Dartmouth College and turn it into Dartmouth University, they were rebuffed in the federal Supreme Court. State courts had held that the college was established for public purposes of a sort that gave the state legitimate authority over it; but the oratory of Daniel Webster persuaded the Supreme Court by a five to one majority that although it was perfectly proper for state governments to establish publicly financed colleges, they could not simply expropriate a private "eleemosynary institution," such as the college clearly was. It is often said that the Dartmouth decision set back the creation of state colleges for some decades and, perhaps more important, opened the door to a flood of tiny, and often short-lived, private colleges. Francis Oakley observes that one of its most important results was the feature of American higher education that most astonishes Europeans: the sheer variety of institutions in which it is carried on, and the vast differences in size, prosperity, and above all intellectual quality.

Today, some fourteen million full- and part-time students attend all sorts of places, from storefront two-year colleges handing out associate degrees to the graduate schools of CalTech and MIT. Rather little of what is on offer is liberal education. In the Ivy League and the liberal arts colleges, 90 percent of students get a traditional liberal arts education; in the entire higher education sector, loosely characterized "business studies" provide two-thirds of the courses. This is a thoroughly modern state of affairs, dating only from the expansion of the 1960s and thereafter. In the first great expansion after the revolution, there was no diminution of concern for liberal education. It was only later, with the rise of agricultural colleges and vocationally oriented state colleges, that the primacy of liberal education came under threat. It is worth recalling yet again that even after the expansion of college education in the late eighteenth and early nineteenth centuries, not many more than one American in a thousand went to college. Even in so classless a society as the United States, those who went were markedly upper-class.

College education was not in the narrow sense vocational, but it was an education for persons whose vocations were tolerably clear—the ministry, law, medicine—or who would be "gentry." It was not merely decorative, ornamental, or a means of self-expression, but it was not narrowly utilitarian. Learning the craft skills of the preacher, doctor, or lawyer happened elsewhere, commonly on the job. The chance to learn how to comport oneself in no matter what learned profession was something colleges could offer. The students were, as they were at Oxford and Cambridge at this time, very young by the standards of a later day. It was common to graduate at the age of eighteen or nineteen; and although boys entered college young, they frequently took only three years to graduate. The tales of assaults on the faculty, pistols fired at night, and frequent near-riots over poor food are reminiscent of what went on at the great English public schools such as Winchester and Westminster in the early years of the nineteenth century, although the religious revivals that swept through American colleges in the early spring were a distinctively American phenomenon. Nothing that we should now recognize as "advanced studies" was possible, nor was it attempted. But this was a society where a man was old at forty-five or fifty, and a boy of fifteen was supposed to comport himself like a man. So it would be wrong to think that colleges like Harvard, Yale, and Princeton were more like modern high schools than they were like modern colleges.

Moreover, in the early- and mid-nineteenth century, there began to be the traffic between American (and English) colleges and German universities that opened the eyes of the Anglo-Saxon world to the possibilities of a deeper scholarship than any practiced in England or the United States. And the grip of the English conception of liberal education naturally weakened in a society whose commitments were so self-consciously and explicitly "republican." Whether the introduction at an early date of such subjects as "navigation" into the curriculum at Yale and Princeton was also evidence of the familiar utilitarianism of American culture may be doubted, on the other hand. Certainly Ralph Waldo Emerson's seminal lecture "The American Scholar," in 1837, urged Americans to strike out on their own behalf and pay less attention to "the courtly muses" of European scholarship; but this was not an argument for a utilitarian, practical, or vocational approach to education. It was an argument for an indigenous philosophy and a self-confident, self-consciously American literature. Ten years earlier, Yale had confronted demands for the elimination of dead languages from the compulsory portion of the undergraduate curriculum. The Yale Report, published in 1829, defended traditional classical education; indeed, it was the most famous defense to be proffered in the pre–Civil War period. Yet the Yale president, Jeremiah Day, did not repudiate modern subjects: besides navigation, Yale taught chemistry, mineralogy, geology, and political economy. What was repudiated was not a particular content but a business-oriented scheme of instruction. Geometry and astronomy had always had a place in a liberal education; at Cambridge, indeed, students were required until the mid-nineteenth century to take the final mathematical exam before they proceeded to study classics. (At Oxford, characteristically, the sequence was the other way around.)

Curricular Conflicts; Poetry and Science

The place where liberal education was—largely—to take place was not much contested. It is accurate enough to think of pre–Civil War American higher education as collegiate, and to date the rise of the research university from the foundation of Johns Hopkins in 1876. Preparatory schools got young men ready for college, and in college they got a liberal education. Just what constituted liberal education was another matter. Moreover, when one knew what the curriculum contained—if that was what the question of what constituted a liberal education meant—that did not answer the further question of what it was *for*. The thought I want to offer, which is only half-original, is that the curriculum embodied an ideal of cultivation that had a clearly religious background, and which has since retained a dilutedly religious quality. I do not so much mean that many American colleges set out to supply one or another Protestant sect with a supply of educated ministers, though they certainly did. An education intended to inculcate "liberal and comprehensive views" was not *narrowly* religious. It was, however, intended to give its beneficiaries something one might call ownership of a distinctively Christian culture. With the retreat of sectarianism and the rise of secular education, the object of devotion was not the truths of biblical Christianity so much as the cultural values embodied in great literature.

Arguments over "the canon" in the last dozen years mimic amusingly the arguments that occurred in the late nineteenth century when modern literature in English was fighting its way into a curriculum where literary studies had always been dominated by the classics. The question whether to substitute *Paradise Lost* for the *Iliad* is not obviously one that must provoke fury, any more than the question whether to save unused bread after the celebration of communion must provoke fury. But churches have remained separated from each other over the reservation of the host, and professors have thought that liberal education stood or fell with the standing of non-vernacular literature. Meanwhile, another argument, elegantly chronicled in Bliss Carnochan's *The Battleground of the Curriculum*, was going on, which was essentially an argument over the merits of specialization versus the virtues of a general education.[6] This could be, and often was, presented as a choice between a general and literary education on the one hand and a deeper, more specialized, and scientific education on the other. This did not raise only the familiar issue of the place of science versus the place of literature in liberal education. It also raised—as early as the 1840s—the question that still puzzles universities and colleges today. A general, literary education is better given by a scholar than by an ignoramus. A literary scholar is—it has optimistically been thought—naturally and happily a teacher; was it so obvious that a scientist, eager to conduct research, would wish also to teach his subject to unskilled neophytes?

To add more confusion to the confused scene, even before the Civil War there were many voices raised in defense of avowedly non-liberal education; and a more narrowly vocational training was indeed provided by the first state colleges devoted to "agricultural and mechanical science." Or, rather, they set out to provide such a training, but until the last quarter of the nineteenth century had an extremely checkered career. For one thing, state legislatures were unwilling to finance them at a reasonable level; even the least luxurious provision for the basic chemistry and biology that a serious interest in scientific farming implied was beyond the imagination of legislators and taxpayers. For another, the enterprise suffered from divided aims. Was it to educate scientifically minded farmers and mechanics, or was it to provide a general education to men who would not enter the learned professions but would earn their living on the land or in business? The first goal did not appeal to practically minded critics who thought that the skills of any occupation were best acquired on the job; the second goal did not appeal to critics of liberal education, since it seemed to be the extension of liberal education to people to whom it would do no good at all. Both versions of the enterprise also suffered from the fact that there were so few high schools available for the potential students at such colleges. Preparatory schools existed to prepare young men to go to college, but precious few public high schools.

CULTURE AND ANXIETY

There were exceptions—Jefferson's beloved University of Virginia was a state university; it was secular; and it provided a variety of courses of study from which students might choose. But even the University of Virginia had terrible difficulty attracting students who could benefit from higher education, and its intellectual standards were for many years lamentably low.

The state colleges as a class of institution were rescued by a combination of circumstances. One was the availability of money after the Morrill Acts of 1862 and 1890 provided a sufficient amount of federal lands to support state colleges, and especially after the second act provided for their receiving predictable annual appropriations. More important, perhaps, they benefited from the general growth of the American economy after the Civil War. It may appear paradoxical, although it is hardly so in fact, that colleges whose origins lay in the need to train scientific farmers and mechanics flourished at just the moment that urban colleges began to flourish, too. In both cases, however, the possibility arose because money became available just at the time that a new clientele arose, one that challenged the traditional belief that college education was only for the elite.

Three other developments are worth noticing before we return to the high theoretical issue of the virtues of science and the virtues of poetry as foundations of a liberal education. The first is the rise of graduate education. Unlike Britain, the United States took to the German model of university education with gusto. What excited American visitors to Germany was the graduate seminar. In the United States, there was nowhere to touch Berlin, Jena,

Tübingen, or Heidelberg; nor was there anywhere where advanced research in medicine could be pursued. To Germany, therefore, went a stream of young men who came back to launch American graduate education, including G. S. Hall, who became the first president of Clark University, Charles W. Eliot, who revitalized Harvard from his appointment in 1869, Andrew White, who created Cornell, and Daniel Gilman, who had the greatest impact of anyone because he made such a success of Johns Hopkins from the moment it opened in 1876. Because so much of modern university education takes place in graduate school, the rise of graduate education is not wholly irrelevant to the question of what a modern liberal education is for and where it can be had. But in its origins, it was part of the revolt against the liberally educating liberal arts college. The first non-honorary Ph.D. was given by Yale in 1860; by 1918, some five hundred a year were being awarded nationally. Late-twentieth-century students will probably not wish to know that John Dewey received a Ph.D. from Johns Hopkins after two years of study—the standard timescale— and that his dissertation took only five weeks of his final semester to write. The modern semi-permanent graduate career is a very recent development, and one that we may hope is already on the way out.

The second is the rise of education for women. In spite of the fact that Oberlin College was coeducational as early as 1833, there was in the first half of the nineteenth century almost no opportunity for women to pursue genuinely post-secondary studies. Most "female seminaries" were essentially high schools, and their intellectual standards unrigorous. Only after the Civil War did matters change, and then quite swiftly. Wellesley, Smith, and Vassar colleges date from the 1860s and 1870s; older establishments such as Mount Holyoke and Bryn Mawr began to raise their standards. Radcliffe and Barnard were established adjacent to Harvard and Columbia, while midwestern and western institutions either became co-educational or began as co-educational institutions from their foundation. Some of the commentary on female education was—appropriately—perfectly hysterical. Men who ought to have known better announced that the effect of excessive study would be neurosis and sterility; racial degeneration would be inevitable if upper-class women undertook studies that would result in their having fewer children than they ought to have for the well-being of the nation.[7] Once again, the relevance of women's education to liberal education is much like that of the movement for state colleges. The public thought that it was pointless to educate either working men or women beyond what the needs of their future careers as workers and wives dictated.

The third is the opening of higher education to black Americans. The usual objection to educating black Americans was, of course, that a man whose role in the world was to hoe and plow had no need of an education at all, let alone higher education. Like most American colleges in their early years, only more so, black colleges were chronically underfunded and usually short-lived. Interestingly enough, two black Americans—Edward Jones and John Russwurm—graduated from Amherst and Bowdoin in 1826, some fifteen years before Oberlin awarded the first three bachelor's degrees to women. Few pre–Civil War black colleges survived into the twentieth century; the best known is Lincoln University in Philadelphia. After the Civil War, the Freedmen's Bureau and a number of northern missionary societies set out to establish colleges for the emancipated Negro population—including Fisk, Morehouse, and Howard. As with those who wanted to found colleges for women, the founders of black colleges wanted to provide for blacks an education indistinguishable from the education that whites found acceptable. The reality, however, was that the inadequacy of the secondary education available to black students was so marked that only Fisk and Howard University were able to teach anything resembling the traditional liberal arts syllabus.

As they did over other aspects of black emancipation, Booker T. Washington and W.E.B. Du Bois quarreled over the conclusions to be drawn from this state of affairs. Washington thought it would be easier to gain white support for black education if the education of black Americans was confined to practical subjects. Du Bois thought that this was a cowardly concession to white prejudice. Again, the relevance of this piece of history to our topic is only that it shows a familiar argument in yet another setting. The one final point to be made is that in the last third of the nineteenth century, the demand for higher education gathered strength. By the time the United States entered World War I, there were 350,000 students in some form of higher education. This was only some 4 percent of the age group, but it was three times as high a percentage as in Britain, and it was a period when only 7 percent of the population went to school after the age of fourteen.

I will pick up the twentieth-century history of higher education as a preface to my final chapter on our present discontent with higher education. I conclude this account of the origins of our contemporary hopes and uncertainties with a last look at the claimed preeminence of literary studies in a liberal education. To do this, I draw on Mill and Arnold, the two preeminent liberals who made "culture" their subject. Mill never had the impact in the United States that he had in Britain and France, but even in an American context he epitomized reforming, public-spirited, secular, and democratic values. Arnold, the purveyor of "sweetness and light," was in both countries contrasted with the man whom Charles Eliot Norton described as an "intellectual iceberg." Those who thought Mill represented "science" and that science stood for progress, preferred the iceberg. In the early 1880s, the students of G. S. Morris at the University of Michigan complained of their diet of German idealism and Christian moral uplift, and expressed the suspicion that their teacher did not tackle Mill and Herbert Spencer because he dared not. Arnold reinforced American anxiety about the uncultured quality of American life, about the hostility of self-made men to "college men," and about the hold of old-fashioned Calvinism on colleges and universities. Both Mill and Arnold had the United States very much in mind while writing about the prospects of late-nineteenth-century Britain, and both saw the United States as the place where the compatibility of liberalism and high culture would be put to the crucial test. Only Arnold ever visited, several times.

To my earlier question whether the term "liberal" means the same when it qualifies "education" as it does when it qualifies "anxieties," Mill and Arnold return different answers. Mill's conception of an adequate liberal education was tailored to his politics. The self-aware, self-creating hero or heroine of *On Liberty* sets the standard by which liberal education is to be judged. Mill took pains to say that such a creature will appreciate many of the things that reflective conservatives have valued, whether this is an appreciation of the natural world, an affection for traditional forms of behavior, or an acceptance of the importance of authority in cultural and intellectual matters. (These attempts to proffer an olive branch to conservatives fell flat; Mill's observation in *Considerations on Representative Government* that the Conservative Party was "by the law of its being, the stupidest party" gave too much offense.)[8] Still, just as Mill insisted in *Representative Government* that democracy had no need of "a party of Order" and "a party of Progress," because order was no more than a precondition of progress, so the "conservative" elements of character are all ingredients in a life built around the ideal of autonomy.

Arnold is harder to pin down. At times he seems to be opposing the values of culture to the values of liberalism; this is certainly true when culture is understood as a subordination of our own judgments to "the best that is thought and written in the world," and liberalism is understood in terms of the laissez-faire enthusiasms of mid-Victorian British governments. This is the Arnold to whom late-twentieth-century defenders of high culture so frequently appeal. They are quieter than Arnold was about the fact that "sweetness and light" are in opposition to commerce and to Protestant self-abnegation; but they approve of his emphasis on the disciplinary effects of high culture. More important, Arnold suggests that it is an inadequate, thin, and ultimately self-destructive liberalism that confines government to matters of economic management—a matter on which he and Mill were as one, though they had different ideas about how governments might express their concern with culture. A concern for the culture of all its people is a proper concern for a liberal political order. On that view, a cultivated liberal is not only a cultivated person but a better liberal. It still remains true, however, that the connection between *education* and *liberalism* is, so to speak, an external one. The cultivation that a liberal education provides corrects and restrains the bleaker and more utilitarian tendencies of the politically liberal mind.

Mill wrote about culture in terms of his famous opposition between Bentham and Coleridge. He painted what he saw as the two main conflicting tendencies of the age as a conflict between two representative figures: the utilitarian philosopher, political theorist, and legal reformer Jeremy Bentham and the poet, philosopher of religion, and cultural critic Samuel Taylor Coleridge. Bentham was, in Mill's eyes, the man who epitomized the eighteenth-century Enlightenment: analytical, reform-minded, critical of existing institutions, contemptuous of what he called "unexamined generalities." Coleridge epitomized the nineteenth century Romantic reaction against this excessive rationalism: discursive, historic-minded, reform-minded, too, but in a conservative fashion that involved recalling the English to their own traditions. In what Bentham had dismissed as unexamined generalities, Coleridge found the deep wisdom of the human race waiting to be elicited. It was true, said Mill, that Coleridge's views on economics were those of an "arrant driveller," but Coleridge's understanding of how a society held together, what its people needed to know, and where it might draw its spiritual sustenance was infinitely superior to Bentham's—indeed, Coleridge understood the subject and to Bentham it was a blank. What Coleridge offered, as Mill well understood, was a theory of culture. It sustained a theory of education, and announced the need for a learned class—what Coleridge coined the term "clerisy" to describe—who could serve the functions of a learned clergy but on a secular, or at least a nonsectarian, basis.

What Mill drew from Coleridge's work was the thought that there might exist a form of cultural authority that would transcend political authority in the narrowest sense, and yet would sustain it, and that would be simultaneously intellectual and emotional. In part, this was to draw on Shelley's well-known claim that poets were the "unacknowledged legislators of mankind"; in part it was to take up Coleridge's insistence that the state could not secure a willing and intelligent obedience unless it embodied a national spirit, a sentiment of unity, and attachment to a particular national culture. This was, though Mill never developed the idea, potentially an elegant way around the problems posed by what was later baptized "multiculturalism." For it allowed a liberal nationalist to acknowledge with pleasure the multiplicity of different cultures in the world and to encourage their expression in a national setting, while also suggesting that a plurality of more local cultures in a society would need some form of appropriate political expression, too. Looking forward from Mill in the 1830s and 1840s to ourselves a century and a half later, it appears that Mill reverses the implications that John Rawls or Ronald Dworkin draw from the fact of cultural plurality. They claim that the state must be "neutral" with respect to all those cultural allegiances that do not themselves amount to attacks on a liberal state. Their reasons are good ones—primarily that state incursions into religious or cultural allegiances cause misery, alienate the victims, and do little good to anyone else. Mill would not have doubted it. He was, however, more ambitious than they, and hoped that an intelligently governed society could weave together what one might term "sub-national" cultural attachments into something that sustained a sense of national identity.

Mill's essays on Bentham and Coleridge were, during the 1950s, part of the canon of exemplary works on the idea of a national culture that F. R. Leavis and, after him, Richard Hoggart and Raymond Williams taught to a generation of mildly left-wing students of English literature. But they never seized the educated imagination in the way that Matthew Arnold's *Culture and Anarchy* did. Written in 1869, it was both blessed and cursed by Arnold's facility with elegant aphorisms. The very title ensures that conservative readers will think the book was written for them rather than for liberals. However, Arnold's intention was essentially liberal and democratic; he wished the blessings of a literary high culture to be extended to the working class. For this to happen, the ruling elite must become cognizant of what cultivation was, and the middle class must raise its eyes from its account books. Arnold hoped to convert the Barbarians and the Philistines for the benefit of the Populace. "Barbarian" was his happy label for the English governing classes, who might profess a muscular

Christianity but might equally profess nothing more than muscularity. They might collect an Empire in a fit of absence of mind and impose a rough-and-ready order on the world, but they could not civilize the estranged proletariat of a modern industrial society, because they had no idea what civilization was. They had no sense of those touchstones of human existence—"the best that is thought and said." The "Philistines" were the middle-class dissenters whose lives rotated around a narrow sense of duty; they were respectable, legalistic, and distrusted pleasure, beauty, and the inspiration of the senses. John Dewey described the Congregational Protestantism of his Vermont childhood in very much these terms, and Arnold himself complained of the impact of dissent on American life in his mean-spirited essay "American Civilization." Political authority in Britain was slowly slipping from the hands of the Barbarians and into those of the Philistines—which is to say that an aristocratic politics was being transformed into a middle-class politics. The leading lights in this movement, thought Arnold, were John Bright and William Cobden. They were pacifist, free-trading, and insular Little Englanders, who, he thought, had no sense of what it might be to be a citizen of the world, to reckon success by noncommercial measures.

Thus far, Mill and Arnold are natural allies. Both, evidently, think of the ideals of liberal education as even more important for an industrial and commercially minded society than for its simpler predecessors. Against the critics of liberal education in nineteenth-century America, who thought a more utilitarian, practical, and vocational education should replace traditional liberal education, their reply is that just because the society offers so many incentives to acquire the vocational and practical skills we require, it is all the more important to balance these pressures by disinterested, non-instrumental, and in that sense impractical instruction. This is an ideal of "cultural literacy" in a stronger sense than that of E. D. Hirsch. What it implies for a modern university education, and for a modern high school education, I shall spend the next two chapters explaining. At the very least, it involves the ability to "read" a poem in a fashion that goes beyond merely stringing the words together and to read a novel in a way that goes beyond merely following the story—and, by extension, the ability to understand how other societies and traditions of interpretation have thought of such things. And in implying this, it suggests the need for more ambitious programs in history, literature, and languages than most high schools and colleges dare to contemplate.

Here, however, I want to end by opening up the question of the place of science in a liberal education and by making some last observations on the kind of liberalism a liberal education might sustain. Surprisingly enough, the two topics are related, and Mill and Arnold show why. Mill's ideal of a liberal education was firmly rooted in an attachment to the classics, as his rectorial address to St. Andrews University insisted. What the classics were to teach was another matter. Mill admired the Athenians for their politics, for the vitality of their citizens' lives, and for their democratic aspirations. Athenians did not confine their interests to a literary education, and they were not superstitious about the wisdom of their ancestors. In short, a concern for the classics was to feed a concern for a lively democratic politics, and for a kind of political and intellectual ambition that Mill thought Victorian Englishmen lacked. It followed that when Mill asked the question whether we should seek an education for citizenship or an education in the classical tradition, he inevitably answered Both, and when he asked whether such an education ought to be a scientific or a literary education he unhesitatingly answered Both once more. These were not Arnold's politics, nor Arnold's educational ideals.

In politics, it suffices to remind ourselves that Mill was unbothered by the protests at the time of the Second Reform Act that terrified Arnold. Mill embraced self-assertion in politics in a way that Arnold could not. Mill was a democrat of a kind Arnold could not be. Arnold's reluctance to embrace the modern world colored their educational differences. Arnold insisted that science could not provide the basis of a liberal education. The capacity for "criticism" to which he thought education should train us up was essentially poetic and literary. It was also, one might complain, very passive. Learning physics or chemistry could hardly be expected to inculcate the kind of sensibility Arnold had in mind. It is all too easy to see why radical professors of literature take Arnold as the representative of everything they dislike. If the study of literature amounts to the establishment of a canon of indispensable work to which we are to pay homage, any red-blooded young person will want to dynamite the study of literature so conceived. Arnold, of course, had a much more complicated view of what the study of literature in a university might involve; he had an almost boundless respect for German scholarship, and for the historical and philological studies for which German universities were famous. The views for which he is best known applied not to higher—or deeper—scholarship, but to the impact of literature on the nonscholarly. In that sense, it is not unfair to juxtapose Arnold's conception of education and a more aggressive modern conception of a radicalizing education.

More interestingly, and more paradoxically, however, Arnold begat the twentieth-century thought that culture is for us what religion was for our forebears by analyzing religion as *essentially* poetry. The effect was first to alienate readers who saw that Arnold was announcing the death of literal Christianity and the futility of sectarian differences, and second to persuade his later admirers that culture was religion. Every commentator has observed that the recent culture wars have been fought in the heresy-hunting spirit of the religious wars of the sixteenth and seventeenth centuries. If the point of culture is to save our souls, whether in a transcendental sense or a more secular one, culture wars are just religious wars. In *The Culture of Complaint*, Robert Hughes mocked Americans for subscribing to the view that art is either religion or therapy, and there is something mad about recent arguments. But it is not willful silliness. We are trapped by ideas put into circulation by the Romantic poets, by Matthew Arnold, and later by T. S. Eliot. The residual effect persists; F. R. Leavis's belief in the potentially redemptive properties of the Cambridge English Tripos (honors examination) is mirrored in every literature department in the United States where "theory" is nowadays thought to yield insights into the human condition that orthodox philosophy, sociology or political science cannot.

What can we learn from this quick foray into the past? Perhaps the *half*-comforting thought that our anxieties and uncertainties are not new. We have been wrestling for a century and a half with the question of what culture a liberal education is to transmit, what the place of science, classical literature, modern literature, history, and linguistic competence in such an education must be. We have for as long been wrestling with the question of how far to sacrifice the pleasures of individual scholarship or deep research to the demands of teaching, just as we have been arguing about what education can achieve, and for whom —whether it is to put a polish on an elite, to open the eyes of the excluded, to permeate society with a secular substitute for the faiths of our ancestors, or to link a new society with an old tradition. The fact that we have been arguing about the same problems for a very long time is only half-comforting, since it suggests that we may not come to anything like a consensus for many years yet. On the other hand, it offers the mild comfort that our condition today is not an especially fallen one, and that even in the absence of general agreement about what we are doing and why, we can do a great deal of good.

2

THE LIBERAL SCHOOL

Liberal and Non-liberal Education

In the United States the emphasis on the importance of the system of public education for the political health of the nation has been greater than in perhaps any country other than France under Napoléon or the Third Republic. Since the United States was the first modern state to base itself on distinctively liberal principles—equality before the law, accountable government resting on the consent of the governed, separation of church and state, and an acceptance of cultural plurality within a unified political order —the principles that the founders relied on the educational system to inculcate in the rising generation were necessarily liberal principles.

Whether a training for liberal citizenship has much to do with liberal education is one of the questions to which this book is devoted. We are perhaps too quick to swallow Thomas Jefferson's rhetoric, and to believe that it must. I have suggested that one view of liberal education answers that question in the affirmative because it looks to an education in self-reliance and autonomy. Literature, history, the natural sciences, and mathematics are tools for the fashioning of character; on that, anyone might agree, whether conservative, liberal, or apolitical. The liberal view has it that this fashioning is *self*-education. As they develop, students achieve an intellectual and cultural mastery, and an ambition for improvement, that must lead to an activist and outgoing social and political style. In an American context, this is a platitude, because the American context is a liberal one. It takes little imagination to see that a different culture might foster instead the idea that a student should learn the things that help him embrace his "station and its duties." Indeed, the English Hegelian philosopher F. H. Bradley urged just that against John Stuart Mill. A more devout culture, or one that imagined a larger public role for religious faith than the U.S. Constitution allows, might emphasize the acceptance of limits, the renunciation of worldly aspiration, the importance of learning inner serenity. Matthew Arnold's liberalism was tempered by such sentiments even when his religious faith had all but vanished.

In the United States, the most obvious challenge to the liberal ideal of education has been posed by a commercial, or, if that sounds too dismissive, a practical, ideal of student competence. The liberal ideal is political; it looks to the creation of good citizens, and in embracing liberal education as a means to that end, it looks to the education of autonomous, argumentative, and tough-minded individuals as the safest and best way of creating good liberal citizens. Simpler sorts of patriotism or less participatory ideals of citizenship would result in very different views of education, though they would all be in this sense political. Economic ideals are at odds with all political ideals. They place the worker, the consumer, and the entrepreneur at the center of the educational process—though they need not entirely dismiss political concerns, of course, any more than a more political ideal need entirely dismiss economic concerns. Here, I largely ignore the view that the most important part of education is fitting students to earn their own living. I ignore it not because it is unimportant, let alone because it is an uncommon view. It is the most common view of the purpose of education, even though the principals of schools and the presidents of colleges do not like to say so very loudly when they graduate their students. I ignore it because I so completely take it for granted that one thing schools and colleges must do is to graduate students who can survive economically. Our subject, however, is not that; I have in the introduction sufficiently paid my respects to the proposition that an education that does not do that much is not an education at all. Our subject now is, rather, what *more* can schools and colleges do?

For that reason much of this chapter focuses on the question of whether the liberalism of educational reformers has undermined traditional liberal education. The thought that it might have done so is simple enough; if liberalism in the classroom fosters a "child-centered" education that leaves it up to the children what they learn, the disciplines of history, foreign languages, mathematics, and the sciences may not appeal to them. What then? It seems that the liberal classroom will be no place for a liberal education. Liberal education is often defined negatively: it is not business education, not vocational training, not technical education. Or, as skeptics sometimes observe, since all education is vocational education, liberal education is vocational education for the superior vocations—law, medicine,

ALAN RYAN

scientific research, teaching (especially in higher education). Traditionally, the association of liberal education with these professions gave it a class character that explains why so many critics in the nineteenth century wanted to replace liberal education with more practical, vocational, or "modern" forms of education. I shall say now what I shall argue for later, that not all students will want or benefit from the full program of a liberal education, though all will benefit from a decent foundation in liberal education, whether or not they like it. It is an interesting, and still an open, question how far an education whose aim is fundamentally technical and vocational can also be a liberal education. As we shall see, one of John Dewey's educational enthusiasms was an enthusiasm for somehow closing the gap between them. It is an enthusiasm worth maintaining.

Positively, liberal education is defined less by its content than by its purpose: the provision of a general intellectual training. This plainly requires a nice balance between the absorption of information and the acquisition of the appropriate skills to use that information. Whether there is a place in liberal education for "learning by rote" is not a question to which a yes or no answer should be returned. There is obviously a great deal of information that is best learned by rote; but a physicist who had done no more than learn a textbook by heart would not be a physicist any more than a student who could recite the *Complete Works* of Shakespeare would thereby qualify as a literary scholar. Indeed, a liberal education ought to inculcate both a respect for facts and some skepticism about the reliability of what is commonly taken to be fact. It is, however, as demanding as any other form of education. That is why the complaint that liberals have crippled liberal education has to be taken seriously. If liberalism subverts intellectual discipline because it subverts all discipline, it obviously subverts liberal education, too.

The pattern of this chapter is simple. I argue that whatever else may have happened in schools in Britain and the United States, it is not their destruction by a deliberate liberal conspiracy. To demonstrate that, I offer some evidence that liberals are chronically divided between two educational ideals, one of them a somewhat antisocial ideal and the other a highly social ideal. Both might be said to promote liberal ideals of citizenship—but in the one case by teaching students to stand outside the concerns of their fellow citizens, in the other by teaching them to embrace those concerns in a properly self-conscious way. Bertrand Russell and John Dewey represent these two ideals rather elegantly, so much of the chapter explains what the educational liberalism of Dewey—more commonly the target of criticism than Russell—actually amounted to. Then I point out how differently, if equally, liberal Russell was. I have an ulterior motive in organizing the discussion in this way. Both in Britain and the United States, commentators credit educational theorists with an implausible power over events. On both sides of the Atlantic, Dewey has been condemned for lowering standards, for inducing a contempt for facts, and for promoting child-centered education. In fact, Dewey had less effect on public education than he is usually credited with or condemned for, and in any event was hostile to exactly the developments he is supposed to have encouraged.[1]

I am more interested in the fact that Dewey's pragmatism, with its assimilation of thinking and doing, seemed to many of his contemporaries to be a shaky basis for liberal education, no matter what the classroom context. Russell was rightly understood by his contemporaries to be a wilder and less mainstream figure than Dewey. When he was refused appointment as a professor of philosophy at City College, New York, in 1940, it was because his teaching was alleged by a complainant to be "lecherous, aphrodisiacal, venerous and unscholarly." This was not a complaint anyone ever thought of directing at Dewey. But Russell's emphasis on liberating children from the fears and inhibitions of their parents certainly frightened his conservative critics. Both men were coherent defenders of liberal education, though it will come as no surprise that Russell's conception of an educated person had decidedly aristocratic overtones while Dewey's was staunchly democratic. Once we understand liberal education on Russell's and Dewey's terms, it becomes obvious that our current system is inadequate— not just in universities, where most people assume liberal education is centered, but in our high schools and elementary schools, where we must lay the foundations for success.

Some History

I begin with a little history, however, because one of the things that bedevils the discussion of education of all kinds, and at all levels, is the previous history of the school systems that actually exist. On the one hand, the past has created institutions with entrenched customs and expectations that can be altered only with great difficulty; on the other, many commentators form their views of what is right and wrong with schools today in the light of a somewhat mythical history. For example, the fact that the modern high school is not what it was seventy-five years ago is a less impressive foundation for a diatribe against modern education when one recalls that 90 percent of fourteen- to eighteen-year-olds attend high school today, against 20 percent then. Even in the area where there is greatest room for unhappiness—the education received by blacks and Hispanics—the data complicate the issue more than they illuminate it. Almost all the schools that have more black students today than they had twenty-five years ago also have lower standards than they did when they were all white or almost all white. It is very far from true that they are worse than the all-black schools during the period of segregation. Indeed, the average performance of black students has been rising steadily during this time, at a faster rate than that of white students; performance still lags behind that of whites, but the gap is closing. The graduation rate of black students is still 10 percent lower than that of white students—and much higher than that of Hispanic students—but it is now as high as the white graduation rate twenty years ago, and it has been rising faster than the white rate.

Again, declining SAT scores may be less convincing evidence of educational deterioration than critics have believed. Certainly the average score has gone down (and then up again) over the past thirty years. This partly reflects the fact that the number of students taking the test has increased enormously, bringing into the test's ambit students who thirty years ago would not have thought of attending college. Whatever the fate of average scores, the number of students with high scores has increased so much that only the top quarter of the Harvard students of 1961 could have made today's cutoff. This does not mean that the Harvard class of 1961 was stupider or worse educated than the Harvard class of 2001; and it does not mean that the Harvard class of 1961 could not have raised its SAT scores rather sharply if it had been required to. It only means that drawing conclusions about progress and deterioration in public education is difficult, and that we need to be fastidious about the comparisons we draw. It is open to anyone to draw up a wish list of things they wish schools would and would not teach—and I end this chapter by doing so. But it is not open to us to pass these off as objective claims about the schools' success or failure.

The background of this chapter however is the way in which liberal ambitions for education have so often run into immovable obstacles—resistance by children and their parents; the impossibility of getting a consensus on the point of education in a multicultural or pluralistic society; resistance by churches, traditional groups, and linguistic minorities; the difficulty of transferring into any setting that the taxpayers will pay for schemes of teaching that work well in experimental situations with tiny classes and a high ratio of well-trained and highly motivated teachers to handpicked students. I should add that in saying that "liberal ambitions for education" have run into such obstacles, I give a misleading impression. *All* attempts at reform have run into these obstacles, but I am interested in liberal reforms. The question of which reforms do, and which reforms do not, "take" and become part of the accepted educational landscape is itself an interesting one—and has recently been given some interesting answers in *Tinkering Toward Utopia*,[2] an unusually relaxed and evenhanded history of the American school.

In 1983, a presidential commission published *A Nation at Risk*, aptly described as "a fire-and-brimstone sermon" on the disastrous intellectual condition of American public schools. It quoted without any skeptical commentary the claim that "for the first time in the history of our country, the educational skills of one generation will not surpass, will not equal, will not even approach, those of their parents."[3] A brief look at the history of public education suggests that such claims are preposterous. It is not so much that they are false (though on any interpretation that makes some sense of the claim, they certainly are) as that they are nonsensical; like is not being compared with like. Such claims beg all the difficult questions: which skills do we think students should have today; how much do we mind about the performance of the best, the average, and the below-average students; how much do we care about the gaps in performance between different social and ethnic groups? It is quite true that fewer schools teach Greek than formerly; but then no schools at all could teach computer science until very recently. Are we to deplore the decline in Greek or celebrate the rise of computer science? Which members of this generation are we comparing with which members of the generation before them?

What such large claims about progress and decay reflect is the wider social anxieties of the time rather than the state of the educational system itself. The language of "crisis" has been employed ever since Horace Mann announced a cultural crisis in the 1840s that only the common school (a public school open to all) could resolve. It is hardly an accident that *A Nation at Risk* concentrated on the *economic* consequences of inadequate public schools; it appeared at a time when the American motor industry could not compete with the Japanese motor industry, Japanese companies were buying up American businesses, and California seemed likely to be covered over with Japanese-owned golf courses. After several years in which the American economy has been strong and the Japanese economy fragile, much less has been heard of the inadequacy of American education. The anxiety that persists, and it certainly does, is over the cost of education, the corruption of inner-city school boards, and the difficulty of raising the standards of the very worst schools to any measurable extent. The average education supplied to the average student is often felt to be expensive and inefficiently delivered, but it is no longer seen as a threat to the country's future.

In the nineteenth century, Americans enthusiastically supported public elementary education—very elementary education. It was often provided in that staple of American fiction, the one-room schoolhouse. One teacher, almost always a woman, taught essentially the same things to a very small number of children—exactly how many depended not only on the size of the town but on how much call for their labor there was at home or on the farm. Literacy under such conditions meant literally being able to read and write. By that standard, the United States became steadily more literate. As long as the United States was primarily a rural society, the one-room schoolhouse was the norm; as late as 1930, there were still 130,000 one-room schools. It is not surprising that historians who resist E. D. Hirsch's view that Americans have become less culturally literate than they once were should point to the fact that today we are hardly willing to describe someone who reads and writes at a seventh-grade level as literate, while a century ago completing third grade was conclusive evidence of literacy.

This does not mean that standards were "low" a hundred years ago. Bare literacy was not to be sneered at. Horace Mann's argument for the common school required only that children emerge from school able to read and write in English. At a time of mass immigration, literacy in that limited sense was an essential tool of socialization and an essential means to transmit the Anglo-Saxon Protestant culture of the United States to newcomers from less favored places. The argument may or may not have been appreciated—or even have been particularly relevant—deep in the countryside, but it made perfect sense. The concern to socialize children into a common national culture has always been at the heart of the American passion for the public education system. The strains of immigration were obviously a more striking reason for this in the United States than in most other countries; but like other countries, the United States also saw a movement of internal migration from countryside to city that placed as much strain on the ability of families to adapt to new surroundings as migration across the Atlantic had done.

If there has been an astonishing continuity in the hopes placed on public education, the institutions of public education themselves have changed dramatically. Little of what we today take for granted in the structure of schools and the careers of their students is more than a century old. The universal practice of separating elementary school children by age and organizing secondary education by graduated work in specialized disciplines took a very long time to get established.[4] The slow pace of change is hardly surprising, seeing how small a proportion of children went to anything other than a one-room school, let alone to secondary school. "In 1900, only half the population five to nineteen years old were enrolled in school; by 1950, this proportion had increased to nearly eight in ten (and by 1990 to more than nine in ten)."[5] Our idea of the proper length of a school year is rather recent, too. We worry that students spend too few days at school, but in 1900, the average school year was 99 days. Today, we complain that the Japanese school year is much longer than the American school year; all the same, American children spend almost twice as long at school each year than they did a hundred years ago. Much of the character of the modern school system is the product of the urbanization of America. Only when schools were of a sufficient size did it make sense to organize students by age in elementary education; so, not surprisingly, the practice developed in the cities after 1870. Only when there were colleges suitable for middle-class children was it sensible to create public high schools. In fact, the growth of public high schools was strikingly slow, and their curriculum wholly dominated by the college curriculum until quite recently. That, too, is unsurprising in the light of the fact that only some 7 percent of the age group went to high school in 1900.

Much else that we take for granted in the structure of schools came about around the time of World War I. It was the Carnegie Foundation for the Advancement of

THE LIBERAL SCHOOL

Teaching that established the assumption that high school and college courses would come in "course units" worth so many credits, and that such units would reflect at secondary level the work done in a period a day for a five-day week. Paradoxically enough, the high school pattern was set not because of a national determination to rationalize the organization of schools but because in 1905 Andrew Carnegie had set up a fund to provide pensions for retired college professors. Deciding what constituted a "real" college focused the foundation's mind on entrance requirements, and thus on a "real" high school curriculum. Essentially, the foundation decided that real colleges required fourteen courses in English, history, mathematics, and science for admission, and schools found it easy to organize themselves around such a structure. Of course, the new pattern was not invented out of the blue. Some moves in this direction had been made already, and the desire to rationalize and departmentalize instruction and to enhance accountability at both secondary and higher levels was very much in the air; it was hardly likely that such fundamental principles of progressivism would affect city governments and the public service and leave education untouched. Still, there remains something curious about the fact that the most immovable feature of high school curricular organization should have had its origins in the need to find pensions for college professors.

Changes in the content of the curriculum reflected the debates of the day in the same way. By the end of the nineteenth century the primacy of traditional liberal education in the narrowest sense was plainly over. It had become impossible to argue that students in college should all take the same courses; it had become impossible to argue that practical subjects had no place in a college education. Institutions that had begun as training schools for teachers were turning themselves into state colleges; and what they tried increasingly to model themselves on was not the New England college of the early nineteenth century but Johns Hopkins or the University of Michigan. The effect on school curricula was to encourage high schools to demote traditional literary subjects from the first rank of studies and to promote not only mathematics and the natural sciences but vocational and technical subjects, too. This process had many effects. One, to which I will shortly return, was to reinforce the movement to divide secondary schooling into academic and vocational streams; paradoxically, however, another was to inspire the teachers of vocational subjects with academic ambitions. If universities were ready to treat domestic science, secretarial training, and the niceties of writing advertising copy as subjects for which students got as much credit toward their degree as they would have gotten for studying Greek or physics, schools could hardly do less.

Liberalism Social and Antisocial

I turn now to the contrast between the two kinds of educational liberalism that I identified earlier. An objection I should dispose of is that neither Russell nor Dewey was a particularly anxious thinker, both were more nearly utopians. They were in fact temperamentally exceedingly different, but neither thought that the achievement of a liberal society would come easily or automatically. Curiously enough, both were brought up by strong-minded women imbued with well-developed senses of sin—in Russell's case, his grandmother, the Countess Russell, and in Dewey's, his mother, Lucinda. When Dewey was born in 1859, it was just nine months after his older brother had died after being horribly scalded; the attentiveness of Dewey's mother to her child's welfare was not to be wondered at.[6] Born in 1872, Russell lost both parents before he was four; many of his relatives were in fragile mental health. His grandmother's attentiveness was not surprising either. Russell's grandmother was a Unitarian; Dewey's mother a Congregationalist who had been a Unitarian as a girl. Both, however, did their best to instill in their charges a firm sense that God was watching their every action.

The effects were very different. Russell retained a strong sense of original sin, and all his life swung uneasily between the hope that rational men might build a heaven on earth and the desperate conviction that human nature was so flawed that they would build a hell instead. Dewey abandoned not only his mother's Christian allegiances but every philosophy that suggested that human nature was fallen. This led him to create a strikingly relaxed and unworried philosophy; nonetheless, Dewey's optimism was *cosmic*, not institutional. He wrote to his long-term friend and correspondent Scudder Klyce that he was a "great optimist about things in general but a pessimist about everything in particular."[7] That was to say that he did not believe in original sin, nor that the world, or human nature, was fundamentally flawed; but he certainly feared that people were pretty incompetent about building a happy social environment for themselves—or even a decent educational system for their children. He never doubted that a well-adjusted society would be a liberal society, nor that well-adjusted individuals would be happy liberal citizens of such a society; but he was certain that such a society could be constructed and such individuals educated only with persistent, intelligent, cooperative effort. At a low point for liberal aspirations in the 1930s, Dewey argued in *Liberalism and Social Action* that between the conservative's attachment to tradition and the Communist's reliance on brute force to bring about utopia, the liberal reliance on "intelligent action" promised progress without bloodshed. That intelligent action would characterize modern politics was not something an intelligent man would take for granted.

Dewey had good reasons for his doubts in his own experience as founder (in 1896) of the University Elementary School at the University in Chicago. This wonderful school—usually known as the Laboratory, or Lab, School because it was started with money originally intended for a psychology lab—was tiny, expensive, and private, and it caused Dewey endless trouble during his seven-year tenure. Dewey's correspondence in his Chicago years is full of worried negotiations with the president of the University of Chicago on the one hand and the philanthropic daughter of farm machinery tycoon Colonel McCormick on the other. Her annual donations of a thousand dollars kept the school going when its president, William Rainey Harpur, would not have done so. I do not mean that Dewey's ideals for the school could be achieved only in an expensive, privately financed setting. Some of them could obviously be more easily attained in the very peculiar setting of the Lab School's early years; persuading teachers to see their teaching as a series of social-psychological experiments comes more easily when your school is in principle a social-psychology laboratory. What could not be transplanted into the public education system was the teacher-student ratio that the Dewey school possessed, and the indefinable ethos that new and experimental schools generate just because they are new and experimental, and everyone in them therefore "special." This is what was later baptized "the Hawthorne effect," when industrial sociologists studying a Western Electric factory in Hawthorne, Massachusetts, discovered that productivity rose when working conditions changed—and rose again when they were changed back. Just being the subjects of attention inspired the workers.

Many of Dewey's ideas transplant readily enough into the public educational arena, however. The most obvious is his belief that an adequate education is an education in "problem solving." Today, indeed, schools are often criticized for having subordinated the acquisition of information to a training in problem solving. It is hardly surprising that a concern for problem solving has animated revisions of the mathematics and science curricula in both Britain and the United States, and no more surprising that such efforts have often been frustrated by the demands of "objective" tests and by the requirements of cheap and undemanding forms of student assessment. Problem solving in Dewey's universe was an open-ended exercise, even if it required a consensus on the problem to be investigated and aimed to achieve a consensus on an adequate explanation. When students are given problem sets by their professors, they are usually being tested on their ability to solve puzzles whose answers are well established.

Russell suffered the reverse of Dewey's fears; he often seemed to think that everything might be repaired if only intelligent and humane people were in charge, but he also observed that nobody ought to run a school who did not have a strong sense of original sin. John Maynard Keynes once mocked Russell's politics: "According to Bertie the world is in a terrible state because people are mad and wicked. Happily, the solution is simple; they must just behave better." During the late 1920s Russell ran an experimental school—Beacon Hill—and spoke from experience. As he recalled, the first attempts to do without school discipline were frustrated when the Bigs bullied the Middles and the Middles bullied the Littles; that Sin was Original he concluded when he found a child putting an open safety pin in the soup. The fearlessness that Russell hoped to inculcate—as did Dewey—was an intellectual fearlessness; but however boldly one thought, one would still discover reasons for anxiety about the prospects of liberalism, both social and intellectual. If human nature did not forbid the ambition to create a society where free spirits cheerfully and intelligently cooperated in creating a lively and high-spirited experiment in political and economic self-government, it provided plenty of reasons to suppose it would not happen easily.

This was why schools mattered so much. If liberal ambitions were to take hold, they must take hold of the young. If liberty was to be offered to the young, it must be offered by teachers who themselves believed in it. If teachers were to do a good job, they must be sustained by parents who themselves hoped that their children could lead more interesting lives than they led. Whether a democratic society would easily embrace this project was another matter entirely. There would not be the same urgency about an education in fearlessness if more people were less inclined to cling to old ideas for comfort, if they were less driven by wishful thinking, and if they were less vulnerable to demagogues. As long as they are anxious, conservative, and easily bamboozled, they will surely vote for illiberal policies. This is why liberals such as Mill and Tocqueville feared that democracy would be inimical to the liberal project. Russell was a liberal of that stripe. Dewey, on the other hand, redefined democracy in the way that recent theorists of "deliberative democracy" have done. Democratic government is government by discussion. An illiberal democracy is not a democracy—even if there is universal suffrage and majority rule. Even the enthusiasts for the idea of deliberative democracy agree, however, that the same problem reappears under a different label: we must try to ensure that real rather than inadequate democracy prevails. No matter the terminology, it is easy to see why liberals must think that education matters.

In the 1950s, and again more recently, Dewey stood accused of preaching and practicing child-centered education. In some ways, the accusation is an odd one: teaching that is not pupil-centered is hardly teaching. But the phrase "child-centered education" had come to possess a particular meaning; it was, among other things, the title of a book on progressive education written by Harold Rugg, a professor at Columbia Teachers College during the 1920s and 1930s and the author of *Rugg's Readers*—social science textbooks that roused the ire of New York state conservatives in 1940–41 because of their unfavorable pic-

ALAN RYAN

ture of the capitalist order and their praise of a social-democratic alternative. What "child-centered" meant in the context of educational theory, then, was a view of education that emphasized teaching children what they were interested in and what they wanted to learn, almost to the exclusion of any determining voice from "above"—from the adult world.

Dewey had distanced himself from such an interpretation of his ideas as early as the early 1900s, and he spent much of his last book on education—*Experience and Education* (1938)—doing the same. He was a friend of Rugg's and defended his textbooks against the wrath of the legislators in New York state, but he did so in much the same spirit as he defended Russell against the Brooklyn judiciary when critics brought suit against Russell's appointment at City College, and defended Leon Trotsky against the orthodox Stalinists of the Communist Party of the United States. He was fastidious about explaining how little he agreed with those he thus befriended—Russell's philosophy was rigid and old-fashioned, Trotsky was illiberal and unrealistic. On education, Dewey said over and over that the concept of child-centered education amounted to the thought that there was no need for teachers in the classroom, and that was just silly. Dewey had no objection to taking advantage of the interests of the child; but anyone who reads *The School and Society* or *The Child and the Curriculum* will see that Dewey had a clear, rather simple view of the stages of intellectual, emotional, and social growth that children would be going through from ages six to eleven and the kind of material they would best be taught at these various points in their growth.

THE LIBERAL SCHOOL

More important, he insisted that the process had to be directed by teachers. Teachers knew, as children could not, the next stage of a child's development. The oddity of Dewey's position was, as so often, that he held two views that are usually thought to be at odds with each other; to do this, he simultaneously shed what are usually thought to be the implications of these views. So he believed that the teacher knew the direction in which the child must grow if she was to become a happy and fulfilled adult; but he also thought that the child had some sort of built-in capacity to follow this path. Unlike those who relied entirely on the child's inner potential, he insisted that the growth of the child was not a natural process, like the growth of a plant. Unlike those who relied entirely on the teacher's superior knowledge, he insisted that education was not a matter of writing a fixed script on the blank paper of the infant mind.

Dewey's enormous success as an educational theorist, if not as a political activist, stemmed from the way that he combined so skillfully the rhetoric of the scientist with that of the preacher. On the one hand, his view of the teacher and the classroom emphasized the efficient transmission of conventional intellectual skills; on the other, he represented the work of the classroom as "God's work," and the teacher was in the process elevated to a highly flattering position as the supreme agent of God's purposes on earth. A famous essay, "My Pedagogic Creed," published in 1895, when Dewey had been at Chicago for only a few months, is a case in point. Of course, if you set a writer to produce his "creed," you should expect something like a creed; but Dewey excelled himself. He announced that he believed that education, the art of "giving shape to human powers and adapting them to social service, is the supreme art; one calling into its service the best of artists; that no insight, sympathy, tact, executive power is too great for such service." His readers would have recognized the implied criticism of Aristotle's claim that politics is the highest art. In conclusion, Dewey spoke of the teacher:

> I believe, finally, that the teacher is engaged, not simply in the training of individuals, but in the formation of the proper social life.
> I believe that every teacher should realize the dignity of his calling; that he is a social servant set apart for the maintenance of proper social order and the securing of the right social growth.
> I believe that in this way the teacher always is the prophet of the true God and the usherer in of the true kingdom of God.[8]

It is easy enough to see why Dewey would have become the hero of teachers, and yet not have a very great impact on the day-to-day organization of the classroom and its curriculum. It was the spiritual renovation of education that he had in mind, even when preaching the need to use the insights of such modern disciplines as educational psychology and educational sociology. The antipathy to "fixed subject-matter" that has looked to later critics all too like an antipathy to factual instruction was no more than an insistence on the need to think flexibly about methods and content in the light of these high ambitions. Exactly what one would teach to children was something he was prepared to allow trained teachers to work out for themselves—so long as they had the high conception of their calling that he thought they should have. We can certainly complain that this makes Dewey rather elusive. But he was surely quite right: the connection between spiritual renovation and the virtues of whole-sentence language teaching or whatever techniques are in or out for the moment is not very close.

It ought, perhaps, to be added that Dewey was not by this stage in his life conventionally religious, and "God" had become a label for whatever it is that holds together those things we find of deepest importance, as he explained forty years later in his little book *A Common Faith*. His view of the teacher as engaged in God's work was wholly consistent with an entirely secular view of the work of the school. Indeed, all his life Dewey interpreted the Bill of Rights to mean that religion had no place in the classroom and that taxpayers could not be called upon to support parochial or other denominational schools, and if there had not been a Bill of Rights, he would have argued (as he did) that organized religion was a divisive force whose influence on education should be minimized. Dewey's secularism, however, was not the secularism of Russell, who thought that Christianity was wholly false and for the most part immoral. Dewey was happy to distinguish between the beneficent and maleficent elements of faith, and to promote the former. The beneficent element in faith was its capacity to sustain cultural and moral unity and self-confidence (without compressing a proper plurality of allegiances in the process), and its maleficent element was its tendency to emphasize dogma and difference and sectarianism.

Dewey thought it was wicked to release children for two hours a day into the hands of whatever denominational teaching their parents wished to provide, even though it was, and still is, the sort of compromise one can imagine an American Supreme Court defending. Sects stressed *differences*, when the aim of a good school was to achieve a willing acceptance of the ideals of American democracy. Dewey's aim was to defend what he thought of as a religi*ous* attitude toward democracy from the divisive effects of particular religi*ons*.

Now, we can get to the heart of Dewey's vision of a liberal education. *The School and Society*—the little book he published in 1899 to give an account of his school and its work—contains some curious diagrams linking the day's activity of the school to the child's home, society, and future development; the diagrams spell out in pictures what Dewey's philosophy spells out in words. The child enters the school at age six or so. He is deeply immersed in family life. If a country child, he has already gotten a clear idea how the family gains a living and where the food and drink they live on come from, and how a farm runs, and so on and so forth. The urban school child has no such background. He needs to be socialized into the modern world that he will be joining. So the first step is to replicate in the school setting something akin to the country child's socialization into the family's working lives. Yet, as always with Dewey, this is not a simple matter. For the aim is not to substitute for an experience that is losing its point anyway, so much as to use an induction into serious work via something closer to make-believe work as a base on which to create the emotional, cultural, and intellectual attachments to the modern world that Dewey prized. Getting children to engage in such activities as growing wheat in a Chicago playground, grinding it, baking it, storing it and the bread they had made from it, selling the bread to one another, and so on generally was not only a way of teaching them some elementary chemistry, some arithmetic, some history, and other "academic" subjects but a way of attaching the social world of the school to the social world outside.

Visitors to Dewey's Lab School sometimes thought that what Dewey had set up was simply a kindergarten. Dewey adopted some Froebelian methods without adopting Froebel's justification of them. Friedrich Froebel, born in 1782, started the kindergarten movement in Thuringia, Germany, in the 1820s. Froebel emphasized the productive use of play; he, of all pedagogical theorists, took most literally the familiar analogy between the work of the teacher and the work of the gardener. He was also a mystic and a pantheist, who ascribed to wooden spheres, pyramids, and cones a spiritual and metaphysical significance that would astonish 1990s play-school leaders. In the 1850s the Prussian government suppressed the kindergarten movement, though this may have been because the minister of education confused Froebel with his socialist nephew of the same name. German immigrants brought the kindergarten ideal with them to America, and many progressively minded middle-class American parents had gotten into the habit of sending their children to kindergartens by the time Dewey went to Chicago. But Dewey was not a member of the kindergarten movement. Froebel emphasized fantasy and unconstrained play. Dewey was interested in weaning the child off childish things and getting him or her ready for entry into the adult world.

The obvious question is what this has to do with liberal education. The answer begins with the fact that Dewey was deeply conscious of the difference between the aspirations of midwestern America in 1900 and those of Europe—or even New England—two centuries earlier. What could be preserved from the ideals of a previous age was the thought that a liberal education was an education for freedom; what could not be preserved was the thought that such an education was to be provided only for gentlemen and that in it classics, literature, and history must hold a privileged place. This was not to say that chemistry should take the place of Greek, and lessons in typing the place of literature. Among Dewey's deepest passions was the desire to close the gap between what the English novelist and critic C. P. Snow described as "the two cultures." He believed all his life that the spirit of science and the spirit of poetry were complementary, not opposed, to each other. This was not wishful thinking but a belief that went to the roots of Dewey's pragmatism. Human beings are not passive recipients of experience but active interpreters; they *make* sense of the world they encounter. Poetry is not merely decorative, and not a piece of pure self-expression; it tells us about the world and ourselves just as science does, though it evidently does so according to different interpretative principles. Though Dewey was not a Froebelian mystic, he wished as ardently as anyone to foster the poetic impulse in the child.

The men and women who made up America's democratic citizens were to be educated so that they could acquire and use all the resources of their culture—scientific, literary, spiritual, and technical. I have no decided position on the plausibility of Dewey's view of the mechanics of the process. It seems clear that a Deweyan school would work well with some temperaments and in some places, and less well with others and elsewhere. On the other hand, it is absolutely clear that Dewey's intention was to give young people the free run of a modern culture—of its science, history, literature, and art. If the modern world was in some sense built on the basis of science, it had its own artistic and literary expression, too. Dewey was, among other things, a close friend of Albert Barnes, the eccentric and irascible millionaire who bought America's greatest collection of late impressionist and post-impressionist paintings, and used them throughout the 1930s and 1940s to teach the formally uneducated and untrained how to look at the world through the eyes of Cézanne or Matisse. This was the education not of a gentleman but of a democrat. Because this was the point on which he diverged so completely from nostalgic defenders of the classical tradition, Dewey emphasized the fact that it was a scientific and forward-looking culture into which children were being inducted. When he was making his case in opposition not to conservatives but to the hard-headed defenders of practical training, he insisted on the poetic and literary values of the modern world, too. In *Art as Experience*, he emphasized the importance of not locking art up in museums; it was too valuable to be stuck in a vault, and too useful to the public to be made a private possession.

Dewey's literary tastes, as distinct from his tastes in pictures, were rather solidly nineteenth century, in fact;

Wordsworth, Emerson, and Whitman fell more easily on his ear than Eliot and Joyce. But he was a close friend of the novelist James Farrell, and had a taste, though not one he discussed, for the modern naturalistic novel. His taste in art was more radical, and was formed not only by Barnes but in the course of talking to Matisse himself. If Dewey's incessant appeal to learning by doing *can* be vulgarized into something narrowly and nearsightedly practical, it plainly was not so vulgarized by him. Dewey's ambitions will, for all that, look implausible to critics who think that he never quite recognized the sheer difficulty that most students—if not those with his wide-ranging intelligence—confront when they try to master either the sciences or the humanities. Some of us might also think that the sober and well-behaved Dewey underestimated the emotional sacrifice that academic self-discipline demands. And there will be many scientists on the one hand and writers and painters on the other who will think that Dewey was simply wrong, and that we must choose *between* cultural possibilities and cannot choose to have them all. Dewey believed that in spite of all evidence to the contrary, modern society could yield everything we truly desired, and thus that socializing students into confident membership of that society was, indeed, God's work.

Was this a man who was bent on lowering standards? One might decently complain that Dewey wanted more than any school system could deliver, if only because the task he set for the school system was embedded in a highly contentious philosophical vision of the world. It is impossible to complain that he made too few demands on children and their teachers. Before he started his Laboratory

School, Dewey wrote a wonderful letter to Ellen Flagg Young, a future superintendent of schools, then working in a normal school (the teacher training colleges of the day). Dewey explained at great length and with innumerable spiraling diagrams how a school year in which children cooked and stored and planted and reaped not only would teach them the rhythm of the seasons, and show them the routines by which societies nourished themselves and kept themselves in being, but would provide the basis for elementary chemistry and for an understanding of such otherwise hard-to-fathom ideas as the similarity of rusting and the results of cooking as like effects of oxidation.

In *The School and Society*, we get the same thought. The young child leaves home for school more attached to home and family than to a more abstract and intellectually organized world. Activities involving growing and reaping and storing and cooking—and making things with textiles, too—would maintain those ties to family and community as well as to the productive life of society. But other activities—not necessarily very distinct from these but focused in a different way—would begin to show the child how to reach out and forward to the more complicated world he would come to inhabit when he left school. In short, the intellectual world is a reflection of and a support for the social world. A liberal social environment demands a liberal education, although, of course, what this implies is an education in the intellectual, social, and cultural skills that future citizens require, not rote-learned Greek.

The startling feature of Dewey's work is therefore not that he throws out liberal education in favor of an emphasis

ALAN RYAN

on practical work but that he makes practice the basis of
a liberal education. This was not just a matter of eliciting
philosophical lessons from gardening, and lessons in chemistry from schoolroom cooking. This was the focus of elementary school, and it is worth recalling yet again that in
Dewey's day 90 percent of American children would not
stay in school beyond the age of fourteen. Although Dewey
had little to say about secondary education in general, he
had a lot to say about the relationship between academic
and vocational education. Essentially, he argued that vocational education must be provided in a form that stressed
its "liberal" aspects. "Mere" vocational education would be
a disaster, and Dewey spent ten years in very public opposition to any idea that the United States should emulate
the German system of separate academic and vocational
secondary schools. The authoritarian Prussians might deliver a compliant workforce to their capitalist employers;
the United States should aim to transcend these class di-
visions and educate young people with an ambition to practice industrial self-government. It might be unclear just
what students were going to learn, but it was always quite
clear *why* they were going to learn it. The issues we started
with—debrutalizing the working class, healing the alienation consequent on secularization, and enabling the average citizen to make coherent and useful contributions to
public life—were the issues that Dewey confronted.

He did so in a more optimistic spirit than Mill or Arnold. There was more than one form of religious estrangement, and he thought that his mother's Congregationalist
piety, with its incessant "Are you right with Jesus, John?,"
had produced in him an "inward laceration" rather than a

conviction of the goodness of God. A world in which children understood how the work they did contributed to the well-being of their fellows—which they could do only where it actually did so—would inspire quite enough religious sentiment to keep its citizens not just loyal but devoted. Supernaturalism was irrational; a religious commitment to one's community was not. By the same token, Dewey thought that the working people of his country were not so much brutalized as baffled; the remedy was not to bathe them in the sweetness and light of Hellenism, as Arnold had suggested, so much as to ensure that the inherited philosophical and literary culture was taught in such a way as to point toward the future rather than to deprecate the present.

Some readers may suspect that this is an evasion of the question of just what Dewey thought children should be taught. If it is an evasion, it is Dewey's own evasion. He never liked to be described as an educator, always retorting that he was a philosopher. For all that he wrote *The Child and the Curriculum*, he was not interested in curricular detail. Because he was concerned with the elementary school almost to the exclusion of any concern for secondary and higher education, he did not speak about the virtues of more and less specialized education. Dewey's own practice as a teacher has always seemed difficult to square with his theory. He appears to have been a wholly unreflective teacher, and he took no interest in either course content or pedagogical technique in the places where he worked. All his working life, he taught entirely orthodox courses in university departments of philosophy—and he taught them badly and boringly, if Sidney Hook's memoirs are to be trusted.[9] According to Dewey's account in *The School and Society*, the Lab School was intended to take education in the usual, or "three R's," sense quite slowly; the first two years were largely devoted to weaning the child off the comforts of home and socializing him into membership of the larger group. Only when he had begun to see the point of skills such as reading, writing, and calculation was he to be faced with the need to learn his three R's. To a British eye, accustomed to seeing children of four learning to read and children of six taught to write essays, Dewey's willingness to wait until children were seven or eight years old to teach them the formal skills of reading, writing, and mathematical calculation seems unambitious. On the other hand, Dewey's account of the theory diverges from his description of what happened to children in their first few days at school: as soon as the children arrived, they first constructed boxes for their pencils, and then learned some basic geometry using the boxes for the purpose. That suggests a much brisker movement toward a more conventional syllabus.

Although it was *The School and Society* that made Dewey's reputation and placed him—he was still not yet forty years old—among the foremost educational thinkers in the country, it was *How We Think*, published in 1910, that best illuminated his thinking about the teaching and learning processes. *How We Think* was Dewey's textbook for teachers; it was a great success, but met a somewhat paradoxical fate. The book attacked rote learning, and argued for an education that taught children whatever made them more apt at problem solving, rather than for a fixed body of truths. Its fate was to be given to trainee teachers, who had to memorize chunks of it and recite them to their instructors, as if it were itself replete with the fixed truths in which its author disbelieved. When people said to Dewey that they feared his work was misunderstood, he replied somewhat enigmatically, "Well, I should hope so." It was not surprising that teacher training colleges used *How We Think* as an instruction manual. It was written as a critique of an existing orthodoxy, the five-stage process of preparation, presentation, comparison, generalization, and application that the followers of Johann Herbart introduced to trainee teachers as the formal steps of instruction. It was no doubt irresistibly tempting to replace one orthodoxy with another.

Johann Herbart was born in 1776 and died in 1834; he was a professor of philosophy, but his hopes for a glittering career were dashed because he was the almost exact contemporary of G.W.F. Hegel and overshadowed by him. Although he turned to the philosophy of education as rather a second best, there was a good reason why Herbart was popular with normal schools. Whatever Herbart's own intentions, his schema, when adjusted by his American disciples, offered a clear structure for the preparation of a lesson, into which most subjects could fit with a bit of pushing and squeezing. It was a friendly schema, too, since Herbart emphasized the need to arouse the pupil's interest before trying to teach him anything. It was therefore denounced as "soft pedagogy" by the tougher types who emphasized *effort*. Dewey thought he could close the gap between hard and soft pedagogy, thinking, plausibly enough, that interest would be aroused in the course of solving problems and that interested children would make the necessary effort. Dewey did not set out to provide a step-by-step sequence of his own to replace Herbart's five steps, but in offering his account of five different steps he made it almost inevitable that they would be thought of as a replacement for the Herbartian sequence. Dewey's steps were "i) a felt difficulty; ii) its location and definition; iii) suggestions of possible solutions; iv) development by reasoning of the bearings of the suggestion; v) further observation and experiment leading to its acceptance or rejection; that is, the conclusion of belief or disbelief."[10]

Dewey's entire theory of thought is implicit in this little statement. Humans are problem-solving creatures; only the discrepancy between the needs of the organism and the environment it confronts rouses the organism to sensation or thought. Education is a matter of sophisticating the process whereby we all acquire beliefs about the world. We are also social creatures, and the apparatus we employ in problem solving is one we share with others and could make no use of without their help.

Democracy and Education, published in 1916, emphasizes the social and interactive side of the story. The title of the book suggests what the contents confirms—that education is to prepare for democratic citizenship. Dewey adjusted his account of democracy in such a way as to make this claim more plausible; democracy is explained as free and equal communication and cooperation rather than anything narrowly defined by voting rules and political answerability. Education, then, aims to achieve a mix of efficiency and self-development—there is to be no sacrifice of the individual to the collectivity, and no privileging of individual self-expression over social obligation. One might de-

cently worry that this obscures some real difficulties—
teaching students that they may have to spend a long time
getting rather little out of a subject if they are to master
it, just as keeping democracy going may require the sacrifice of immediate and short-term wishes. Dewey believed
that he could do justice to such anxieties; he emphasized
that working our way through his five steps of learning
requires self-control—we must resist the temptation to
adopt the first plausible explanation we come across, we
must make ourselves look at more evidence than we want
to, especially if it threatens to overturn our favorite beliefs.
Dewey did not believe that education could be painless.

Dewey's Relevance Today

Still, one may think, this is pretty remote from the inner-
city school of the 1990s. In 1995, two New York City
high schools were scheduled for closing; one had managed
to graduate 146 children in the previous year, out of a total
enrollment of 2,400, and the other was hardly better. Both
were plagued by violence; both were plagued by teenage
pregnancy. Does Dewey speak to such a world? Another
problem that plagues contemporary education is the demand for multicultural education. Afrocentric curricula
have been developed in several cities, and they have been
unimpressive—one in Washington, D.C., was developed
by a woman who had just awarded herself an M.A. in curriculum design, having shortly before that turned herself
into a self-validated institute for Afrocentric education with
the power to award diplomas. Does Dewey speak to that?

He does. In Dewey's day as much as in ours, children

slogged their way through or walked out on education that appeared pointless or useless to them. Dropping out early was less of an academic disaster ninety years ago, when fewer than one child in ten went on to high school, but it was an economic disaster for the children who went to work in dead-end jobs from the age of twelve or thirteen. What could be done about it was not obvious. Their parents were too poor to do without their wages, and the thought that the children might engage in high-level intellectual work seemed absurd to most commentators. Reformers with whom Dewey was in sympathy had two things to say. The first was to insist on the value of serious vocational education. The great advocate of this was William Wirth, the superintendent of schools in Gary, Indiana, just before World War I. He is mostly remembered as the inventor of the "platoon" system, by which a school can process twice as many children as usual—by staggering the school day, all the rooms in a school could be kept in use all the time. At a time when building costs were higher relative to teachers' wages than they are today, the savings were impressive. Wirth was more impressed by the fact that—on his own account at least—the students were capable of building, repairing, cleaning, and managing their own schools. Dewey agreed with Wirth that vocational education was part of the solution; but true to his philosophical ideals, he insisted that it must be "meaningful" rather than merely technical.

The thought that education could be vocational and liberal simultaneously seems idealistic. Yet if we focus on Dewey's emphasis on children working in groups, so as to learn to identify and work out cooperative solutions to problems, something applicable to our own anxieties emerges. A few years ago, a mathematics professor at Berkeley, depressed at the poor performance of his African-American students and impressed with the good performance of his Asian-American students, set out to isolate the reasons for the discrepancies. He discovered that his black students studied in an isolated fashion, that they believed they were being judged on individual ability, and that they should not seek help or offer it. The Asian students formed study circles, traded ideas, worked their way from simpler to harder problems, and pulled up the weaker students even while the weaker ones helped the stronger. When these methods were tried by the black students, their grades rose rapidly. The same techniques apply even more simply to vocational education. All very "Deweyan."

The second element in reactions ninety years ago has also lost none of its point. Dewey never supposed that a school could take children out of a battle zone in which family life had virtually ceased and turn them into rational, farsighted, and public-spirited citizens. Neither he nor anyone else ought to be asked to repair in the classroom the emotional and physical damage done outside it. The common error made by readers of Dewey is to suppose that he wanted to socialize children into the American society that existed outside the school. Dewey's aim always was to socialize children into an American society that could be created by radical political and economic change. Dewey thought the New Deal was much too timid, and Roosevelt not so much an experimenter as a bewildered politician thrashing about and trying "a little bit of this and a little bit of that." Education is a matter of transmitting a society's ideals and culture to its offspring. Dewey would have taken it for granted that a society that has allowed its inner cities to decay to the degree that some—though not in numerical terms a great many—American cities have now done must spend its money repairing that social damage before it can do anything useful in the classroom. Dewey would have been the first to say that to hand on the American ideal of equal opportunity, free self-expression, and democratic self-government to children whose lives are at risk from drug dealers, incompetent mothers, drive-by shooters, and the rest is both impossible and a sort of insult. One can't blame teachers for failing to do what political ineptitude makes it impossible to do.

As to multiculturalism, Dewey took it for granted; his Chicago and New York were cities where two-thirds of the residents were either foreign-born or the children of immigrants. Ethnic separatism, on the other hand, he would have thought quite mad. He didn't care for the metaphor of the melting pot, but even the notion of a "gorgeous mosaic," to quote Mayor David Dinkins's optimistic anti–melting pot metaphor, would not do. The idea of separate cultures, lying side by side, was not what he wanted, however gorgeous they might look to an outside observer. He believed much more nearly in a conversational pluralism of cultures. He certainly thought that there was a national American culture to which everyone ought to have access; at the crudest level, this meant that immigrants had to learn English and correspondingly they had to be able to learn it at public expense and in a useful form. "Hyphenated" Americans caused him no anxiety, as long as the hyphen joined rather than separated. He would have had no difficulty with the idea of French Canadians; but he would have had sharp things to say about the folly of linguistic isolationism. It is interesting to speculate on what he might have said about the Québecois insistence on the "distinctness" of Quebec—would he consider this "apart" thinking or a new voice in the conversation?

Specifically *racial* prejudice and separation was something he never wrote much about. He took it for granted that the segregation, legal bullying, disenfranchisement, and lynchings that disfigured the American South were a wicked letdown of the ideals that animated the United States. What he never asked was the question that haunts us: whether the color line is simply harder to cross than any other. In Dewey's day, southern Europeans, Polish Jews, and occasionally the Irish were often written off as members of an inferior "race," and a good deal of ignorant semi-science was devoted to classifying the ways in which they all fell short of the Anglo-Saxon ideal. The refutation of the pseudo science was provided by the economic success of these inferior peoples; when they made money, moved into better houses, and their children learned standard English, their measured IQs rose as well, and their origins vanished from sight. But African Americans can never obscure their color.

The Antisocial Russell

Dewey is a persuasive writer. Or, rather, he is persuasive if we are willing to accept the philosophical premises of his politics. Given those, the stark oppositions in which other writers deal can be softened. There is no conflict between a liberal education and a vocational education, because when both are provided in a form adequate to our world —if not to the class-ridden society of Victorian Britain— they are variations on each other. There is no contradiction between an emphasis on the classics and an emphasis on the sciences, because if we are to employ what Dewey calls "the funded capital" of our culture, we must be able to reach back into its history and understand the modern view of the world as well. There is no contradiction between acquiring a sense of ownership of "our" culture and accepting a multicultural world, because the genius of the United States particularly, but of modernity more generally, is to embrace the resources of humanity, not those of a small tribe. This is not a Pollyannaish view. Students who have the good luck to encounter the kind of teachers I had may never have encountered Dewey's rationale for their education—nor may their teachers, for that matter— but they will have encountered the ambition.

Still, Dewey's is not the only form of twentieth-century educational liberalism, and it is worth considering one alternative vision. Bertrand Russell was as far superior to Dewey as a writer as he was inferior to him in patience, in steadiness of judgment, and in common sense. Although their politics were not dissimilar much of the time, the rhetorical undercurrents of their work were strikingly different. Dewey, for instance, never wrote a word on sex education; Russell wrote a great many, and, indeed received the Nobel Prize in Literature in 1951 largely on the strength of *Marriage and Morals*. This was not merely a reflection of their different tastes and interests. Russell thought of the sources of happiness as essentially private.

He wanted a liberal education—or a liberal's education—
to protect us from the damage that the world can do to
us, while Dewey wanted it to help us to join in the world's
affairs. Russell constantly preached the need for education
to create an intellectual and emotional fearlessness in children; when he wrote most eloquently about the importance
of education for girls, it was when he denounced teachers
who wanted to protect girls, to make them respectable, and
therefore to keep them ignorant and timid.

Russell preached the liberalism of aristocratic individu-
ality, Dewey the liberalism of democratic communitar-
ianism. Both of these creeds were liberalisms, both were
sophisticated and intelligent political and social positions;
they result in surprisingly similar prescriptions for at least
part of the schooling process. As much as Dewey, Russell
proposed to teach children in small groups, to have them
cooperate on projects, to launch out from what they already
understand into new areas in an essentially problem-solving
frame of mind. But the two men were emotionally, culturally, and imaginatively at odds. This bears directly on
the anxieties about the place of high culture and of those
disciplines whose interest lies in their difficulty, complex-
ity, logical rigor, and inaccessibility that readers of Dewey
often express. They fear that for all his good intentions,
Dewey would shortchange the glories of our intellectual
tradition, while Russell would not.

Critics of Dewey could hardly complain that his teaching
was lecherous, aphrodisiac and unscholarly, but they could
complain that he did not take the pursuit of truth absolutely seriously. In this, they would have been on Russell's
side. Unlike contemporary admirers of Dewey such as

Richard Rorty, Russell thought that Dewey's refusal to believe in an objective, impersonal truth—a refusal that is the essence of pragmatism—meant that he could not take intellectual and aesthetic discipline seriously enough. For Russell, the truths of mathematics, the beauty of the sea and the mountains and the impersonal heavens above were essentially a refuge from the messiness and miseries of everyday life. A concern for them is one of the glories of a civilized life, but it is a disinterested concern, and the sense in which it is one of the concerns of a free person is almost Stoic—it liberates us from ourselves and from our practical concerns. One of the things he felt about the sea, the mountains, and higher mathematics was that they did not mind about us, they were beyond usefulness—and that was why they mattered. Comically enough, both he and Dewey leveled the charge of "impiety" against each other—Russell because he thought Dewey's obsession with making use of the world implicated the cosmos in humanity's squalid affairs, and Dewey because he thought Russell's emphasis on the cold impersonality of what he most valued was a sort of insult to a world that Dewey thought essentially friendly to human purposes.

My heart is with Russell. Russell's exhortation to his readers to mind about those things that do not mind about us catches something that is otherwise hard to describe about the way individuals find their own intellectual and emotional allegiances, and find a particular pleasure in the experience of intellectual difficulty. Dewey never denied that there were intellectual standards; people who criticized him for preferring "life adjustment" to high intellectual standards got him wrong. Still, Dewey had no vocabulary for describing the pleasures of mastering a difficult subject and he had nothing to say about the emulative and competitive pleasures of the intellectual chase. Indeed, his readers may not be wrong in thinking that he would have preferred not to know about intellectual competition and emulation. If so, he was too much in tune with the public, in his own day and ours. The moral, however, is what I began with.

Dewey and Russell were impeccable liberals; they were concerned with educating liberals, and with liberal education; both lost interest in the content of education at the stage where students ought, if properly taught, to be able to start learning difficult subjects for themselves; both thought that unless good foundations were laid early on, the outlook for students in their teens was gloomy. Since recent British research suggests that more than 70 percent of students' performance at fifteen is predictable by the time they are seven, their predilections were more than justified. Dewey and Russell were also utterly different sorts of liberal. Still, it might be complained by a last-ditch critic, their hopes for elementary school reform have triumphed, and the results are surely dreadful, so it is true that liberals have destroyed pre-college teaching and education.

Utopia

The answer is that what has triumphed is only the common core of methods in very early teaching that almost every educational theorist of the nineteenth and early twentieth centuries advocated. Nobody watching four- or five-year-old children at work today—in Britain and the United States, at least—could infer the political and philosophical allegiances of the teachers, the local school board or education authority, or the children's parents. As to the dreadfulness of the results, these are, like the death of Mark Twain, greatly exaggerated. There are certainly many things that many children could once do that most late-twentieth-century children cannot. These are commonly things that require a good deal of memorization—reciting long poems, dashing off the multiplication tables in one headlong rush, listing the kings and queens of England and the capitals of all the American states. Because there is less agreement on what a good high school education consists of, there are some other skills much less in evidence. Almost no school child in Britain could today write Greek verse, whereas the great-grandfathers of many of them could have done it badly at the age of twelve and quite decently at eighteen. It is not clear what other intellectual tasks are performed less well. Music, chess, painting flourish where there are resources; and while American high schools fear they are not educating students as well as Japanese high schools, Japanese high schools wish to be more like American schools.

This is not utopia, so what would the liberal educational utopia look like? When Dewey wrote an essay for *The New York Times* entitled "Schools in Utopia," he began with the promising remark, "In utopia there would be no schools."[11] Teachers, as he had remarked forty years before, were society's servants "set apart" for a purpose. In utopia, there would be no separation of institutional arrangements and, so, no schools. One might think this is going too far. The first thing to say about schooling in utopia, however, is that most of it would happen somewhere other than at school. In utopia, there would not be a Head Start program, because nobody would need a head start; or, to put it another way, everyone would have a head start because all children would be wanted, parents would be competent, and, barring accident, children would be brought up to be sociable, cooperative, lively, and inquisitive. It is not an accident that educational liberals have always been enthusiasts for urban planning, public health reform, birth control, and parent education. Really bad teaching can stifle the curiosity of the happiest child, but an elementary school that is guaranteed healthy and lively children would face few of the problems that demoralize teachers in the first place.

The utopian elementary school classroom is impossible to describe, though not to create. It is impossible to describe because anyone who has ever watched a successful play-group will remember the ebb and flow of children's interest in cooperative and individual activities, and the speed with which children will turn their attention from a strenuous physical activity such as climbing the monkey bars to quietly listening to a story or beginning to puzzle out the meaning of the words in their first reader. The story of the elementary school in utopia is Dewey's story; it is a matter of equipping children with longer attention spans, more patience, and a more self-conscious understanding of the problem-solving skills they are gaining. One thing that Dewey and Russell underestimated, perhaps because they took it too much for granted, is the importance of imitation. Talking of teachers as "role models" puts too pompous a gloss on what every teacher knows; their every mannerism, quirk, facial expression, and tone of voice is affectionately or disparagingly mimicked by their pupils.

Trading on this to get children to mimic literary productions, too, is an obvious element in good teaching. A child who learns how to mimic the prose of the King James Bible, or the poetry of Robert Frost, or the manic stories of Roald Dahl has gone a long way toward learning how to make the English language say what he wants it to say in just the right way. How much rote learning this involves is essentially an experimental question. It may be quite a lot, because it may be that simply accumulating enough English or French grammar and enough mathematical facility to read, write, and calculate requires a good deal of rote learning. It will certainly require the absorption of a great deal of factual information. It ought to involve a lot of foreign language learning, simply because childhood is when it is easiest to learn foreign languages, and children ought to learn how to write clear expository prose almost as soon as they learn to write at all. "Cultural literacy," one might hope, would also be an unknown expression in utopia; children who talk (and listen) to their parents would surely acquire it without noticing.

The utopian high school would foster a plurality of taste and ambition. It is foolish if nobody learns Greek at high school just because not everyone can or should, and what goes for Greek goes for art history, philosophy, biochemistry, and a great deal else—including sailing, rock climbing, and orienteering. Even in utopia, it is likely that many students will learn difficult subjects indirectly—that they will learn trigonometry when they have to set a compass course allowing for wind and tide. In utopia, the well-adjusted teenager knows that in ten years time there will be a serious career to embark on, and will work out for herself what this means for the subjects she would be wise to pursue at school; it is unlikely to mean a diet of business studies, though some students may satisfy Dewey's wish for a liberal vocational education by taking courses that will surely not include business English as presently taught. One thing it might well mean is that students would understand that most occupations they might undertake leave a lot of latitude in what they must study in high school, though we may hope that they would also appreciate that a career in the Parisian theater would require fluent French and a career as a research physicist would require fluent calculus.

I trust that some readers are complaining that this does not in fact depict an educational utopia. The best existing schools already do much of what I have described with children who have been adequately prepared; and there are many families that supply at home what schools do not and complement what schools do give. The utopian element is the thought that everyone might receive such an education, and that the classroom might replicate the talkative family breakfast table. A brief reflection on utopia serves a useful purpose, however. It reminds us how far our educational discontents ought properly to be focused on something other than the classroom—on the family, on the provision of public libraries, on safety in the streets, on the employment market. But it also reminds us that even our best schools are less ambitious than they should be.

Think how wasteful of talent most modern societies really are. We start children too late in school, especially in the United States; almost everywhere we teach them to read and write too late, while the English-speaking countries don't teach children foreign languages when they could learn them most easily. Outside South Korea, Singapore, Hong Kong, and Japan, we do not teach mathematical skills in such a way that children learn the general problem-solving aspects of the subject while learning mechanical procedures in the same way they learn to ride a bike. We don't encourage them to get lost in poetry and imaginative literature, and not because we have allowed them to get too interested in the world of politics and public policy— since we don't do a very good job of teaching them that either. We have become feeble about teaching the history of religion from a secular perspective, and the result is that few school students have any grasp of the place of the Bible in their literary and political inheritance. Teaching such students art history, philosophy, political theory, or the political history of most North Atlantic countries is slow and painful in consequence. Finally, we waste so much time in adolescence that 50 percent of a student's time in British and American higher education amounts to remedial education. It is no wonder that so few students acquire the sense of cultural ownership that liberal education can provide. Happily, youthful curiosity and energy and the spontaneous enthusiasms of their teachers carry a surprising number of them onto better things. One further thing that would help would be for colleges and universities to make more stringent demands of secondary school students. To the supposed loss of standards in higher education, I now turn.

IS HIGHER EDUCATION A FRAUD?

I have spent all my working life in universities on both sides of the Atlantic, with visits to most of the rest of the English-speaking world, and shorter excursions elsewhere. To say that I have never had reason to regret my choice of occupation would be absurd. I have often been bored, have sometimes had to teach students who were idle and obnoxious; I have had a few colleagues whose mere physical presence was enough to drive any rational person wild with irritation. Spread over thirty-five years, this is the small change of a vocation. Most of my colleagues have been hardworking, clever, amusing, and interesting; and most of my students have been a pleasure to teach. In short, I cannot imagine that I would on balance have been happier in any other occupation. On the other hand, neither in the United States nor in Britain is higher education in an entirely healthy state, and I am sure that I would have been happier yet if my profession had been healthier.

The sense of working in a beleaguered system is one I have lived with for most of my career; in Britain, the boom years of the early 1960s gave way to a quarter-century of increasingly underfunded education, where successive governments insisted year by year that we should always do more with less. In the United States, the fact that funding does not come from only one source to the entire higher

ALAN RYAN

education system means that the uniform misery that so
often envelops British higher education is not a problem.
Still, anyone who has worked in the City University of New
York for the past decade, or in the University of California
system during most of that time, will have had much the
same experience as his or her British colleagues—shrinking
departments, frozen salaries, and increased student numbers
facing diminishing resources for teaching, libraries, and
general support. I focus not on that, which is the common
lot of those employed in publicly funded institutions at a
time when the public is reluctant to pay taxes for public
provision, but on something that has affected institutions
in easier financial circumstances as much as in worse-off
places. That is the conviction that there is something educationally amiss, that if colleges and universities were better funded, they would not do a much better job. The form
that conviction takes is very varied. In part, it is like the
conviction that schoolteachers work less and less diligently
for larger and larger salaries. Property taxes rise relentlessly,
but schools get no better; tuition fees rise relentlessly, but
college graduates are no more employable. In part, it focuses more narrowly on curricular and educational issues:
there is a widespread sense, on the one hand, that higher
education teaches nothing that will be useful to students
in later life, and, on the other, that it is so addicted to
teaching useful subjects that liberal education is neglected.

I focus here on two topics. The first is the fate of colleges
and universities as liberal institutions, by which I mean
their success or failure in remaining places attached to
ideals of freedom of inquiry and cultural openness, and
places that take seriously their duty to encourage good cit-

izenship among their students. The second is the fate of traditional liberal education in this context. And as in the last chapter, I begin with a little history, catching up the story I embarked on in chapter 1.

Huge and Complex

Today, the U.S. higher education system educates about 14.5 million students—equivalent to two-thirds of the entire population of Australia. They are looked after by about 760,000 full- and part-time teachers, some 600,000 of whom hold some kind of professorial rank. (The English higher education sector, by contrast, numbered until 1992 fewer than 600,000, students and teachers combined.) Of the 14.5 million students, the majority are women; 45 percent are mature students—that is, over the age of twenty-four; and a bare majority are part-time students, who form a minority in four-year institutions and a substantial majority in two-year institutions. Whereas one hundred and fifty years ago "college education" meant eighteen-year-old white boys attending liberal arts colleges, today such students are a small minority. The number of post-secondary institutions has risen sharply, to around 3,500. They run all the way from Harvard (5,500 undergraduates), or Williams (2,000) to Miami-Dade Community College (40,000, by now mostly Spanish-speaking, students pursuing everything *except* degree-level courses). They include enormous state institutions like Ohio State University, with 34,000 full-time and 6,500 part-time undergraduates, 13,000 full- and part-time graduate students, and 4,000 faculty on the Columbus campus—not to mention people doing M.B.A.s,

J.D.s, M.D.s, and other professional courses, and another thousand students in two-year starter courses at tiny branch campuses.

Our colleges today are denominational and nondenominational; they include "traditionally black" institutions, schools of fine art, fashion, music, and hotel keeping. Among the numbers worth bearing in mind, one is that public institutions represent only about half the total number of institutions offering post-secondary education but account for 80 percent of the students. As that suggests, the average size of public schools is very much greater than that of private schools. But another number worth bearing in mind is that of the 1,841 private or independent schools that the Carnegie Foundation classified in the late 1980s, only about 220 were liberal arts colleges. The thought that public institutions will be offering vocational courses and private institutions liberal education cannot survive the fact that almost 600 private schools are classified as professional schools and another 400 as community, junior, and technical colleges.

It is a matter of nice judgment whether we should think of the growth of American higher education as a twentieth-century phenomenon, or as something characteristic of the 1960s. It is tempting to suggest that during a period of rapid but not explosive growth, higher education was relatively untroubled, and that it has been the explosive growth of the past thirty years that has brought controversies over just about every aspect of it—curricular content, intellectual standards, the faculty's willingness and competence to teach students what they need to know, the cost of an adequate education, the system's commitment to the values of free speech, selection on merit, cultural inclusiveness, and much more. Certainly the expansion of higher education during the first fifty years of this century was striking. "Numbers of students enrolled in postsecondary education doubled about every fifteen years or so, as did the numbers of faculty employed in colleges and universities. Graduate education grew even faster, with the number of earned Ph.D.s doubling every eleven years."[1] The effect was that in 1900, 29,000 students secured degrees, and in 1950, almost half a million. To many of us, however, the more striking phenomenon was the sudden acceleration of this process in the 1960s. It is striking not least because it parallels the sudden acceleration in several other indicators—this time indicators of social upheaval such as the divorce rate and the percentage of babies born out of wedlock. In 1960, there were 2,026 institutions of post-secondary education in the United States, itself an astonishing number by the standards of every other country on earth; but only thirty years later, the number had nearly doubled, with most of the growth coming in the first fifteen years. The growth in the number of institutions is nothing compared with the growth in the number of students, however, and here too almost all of the leap from three and a half million to thirteen million enrollments between 1960 and 1990 took place in the first dozen years of the period. It was, at the same time, anything but "more of the same," as far as demographics, curriculum, and organization went. The percentage of minority students quadrupled—from 4 percent of the student body to 18 percent—the percentage of women rose from 37 to 54 percent and that of part-timers from 30 to 43 percent. And what they studied changed dramatically, too.

The great gainer from the change has been business studies. Conversely, the great losers have been traditional arts and sciences programs. Between 1968 and 1986, B.A.s in arts and sciences went down from 47 percent of all degrees awarded to 26 percent; particular subjects did very badly—in English, the drop was from 7.6 percent to 2.6 percent. Conversely, business degrees had been only a third as numerous as degrees in the arts and sciences, and are now equally numerous. It is not a surprising trend. The coincidence of rising divorce rates, rising rates of labor force participation for women, rising numbers of female, minority, part-time, and mature students would hardly be likely to sustain an increase in non-vocational education. It tends, of course, to give color to the thought that in expanding higher education we have lost sight of what its distinctive virtues and values are. Those who think that what makes higher education higher is its adherence to the verities according to Arnold must view the scene with considerable unhappiness. There is a more cheerful view, however. Given the enormous increase in the numbers of students attending some institution of post-secondary education, falling percentages obscure the fact that the *number* of students getting some exposure to a liberal education is rising rather than falling. More students than ever are getting what is at present the best undergraduate education in the world. The number of students attending the very best liberal arts colleges has risen sharply since the 1960s, as those colleges have struggled to accommodate more students without losing their distinctive character. The numbers in the under-graduate colleges of the Ivy League and its peers have risen in the same way. That there are very many places where what students get can only by courtesy be called a higher education is certainly, and sadly, true. Their existence has not, and does not, undermine the credibility of the education on offer elsewhere.

Past Unhappiness

There are four famous tracts on American universities: Thorstein Veblen's *The Higher Learning in America*; Abraham Flexner's *Universities*; Robert Maynard Hutchins's *The Higher Learning in America*; and Clark Kerr's *The Uses of the University*. The last is the least elegant, and the only one that breathes a spirit of optimism and anticipation. Kerr's predecessors, of whom the first was a radical, anti-establishment economist and sociologist and the other two radical in their educational views but otherwise decidedly members of the establishment, were eager to throw out most of what went on and goes on in an American university. In the case of Veblen and Flexner, it was because they were convinced that what universities were for was the pursuit of knowledge rather than its transmission to undergraduates. They came very close to arguing that a university should have no students at all—so it is not entirely surprising that in 1932 Flexner became the first director of the Institute for Advanced Study in Princeton, nor that Veblen tried very hard to drive even the most devoted students out of his classes. By the same token, their views are almost wholly irrelevant to my purposes. Perhaps there ought to be more research institutes, but whatever they might promote, it would not be liberal education. Their relevance to our topic is, briefly, twofold.

On the one hand, a liberal education ought to give students some taste for, and understanding of, intellectual inquiry conducted at the highest possible level. In that context, it is an important fact that a large percentage of the students from liberal arts colleges such as Swarthmore and Williams go on to do graduate work not only in the humanities but in the natural sciences, too. One might think that Veblen and Flexner could have paid more attention to the fact that teachers in undergraduate colleges will need some experience of, and perhaps some continuing access to, institutions whose primary purpose is research if they are to transmit their values to the undergraduate student. It is otherwise faintly mysterious whence new generations of researchers are to be drawn. On the other hand, research culture is characteristically inimical to the liberalism that I have been suggesting we want liberal education to promote. Disciplined research teams have more in common with well-conducted military organizations than with debating societies. Thomas S. Kuhn's devastating little book *The Structure of Scientific Revolutions* put paid once and for all to the idea that the practice of "cutting-edge" science involves a great deal of open debate and wide-ranging discussion. Save when the entire explanatory framework is under threat, what most scientists do is very difficult and very meticulous, but devoted to filling in gaps in jigsaws whose general outlines are unchallenged.

Hutchins's splendid little tract, on the other hand, really

was concerned with liberal education. Although *The Higher Learning in America* was not the occasion for his defense of an undergraduate education built around the Great Books, it was the occasion for his memorable insistence on the place of the classics in the undergraduate syllabus, and for the unchangeability of the values that underlay such a syllabus—"Teaching means knowledge and knowledge means truth; and truth is the same at all times and places."[2] Given that Hutchins was the president of the University of Chicago, and a very young president at that—only twenty-nine years old when appointed—it was a bold argument. It was directed not so much at the other ornament of the University of Chicago, John Dewey, as at the *image* of a modern, relativist philosophy, prepared to defend neither the objectivity of truth on the one hand nor the permanence of moral values on the other.

But Hutchins, too, wanted to draw a sharp line between the studies proper to undergraduates and the research work proper to professors, in effect preserving the liberal arts college by separating it out from the research university devoted to the higher learning. In many universities, this has been achieved in some form or other; the undergraduate colleges at Harvard, Yale, Columbia, the University of Pennsylvania, and Chicago, for example, are essentially large liberal arts colleges encapsulated within the larger university. At Princeton, the balance remains firmly in favor of the undergraduate college, just as it does in the two British examples of the same way of preserving undergraduate liberal education, the so-called ancient universities of Oxford and Cambridge. The unanswered question is

[151]

ALAN RYAN

whether what is now offered in such places is a liberal education in the two senses we have been examining thus far. To that question I now turn.

Present Discontents

I start with an alarming paradox. The population entering higher education is enormous, yet the higher education system is highly unpopular. Why innumerable students wish to get an education that so many commentators assure them is overpriced, inadequate, and delivered by idle ignoramuses is deeply mysterious. The job of a university president in the United States is an increasingly well paid one—the presidents of major universities are paid $250,000 and up, with cars, houses, and pension plans to match—but it is also an increasingly stressful one; many presidents resign within a year or two of arrival, and the average tenure lately is in the region of five years. This really is one area in which a golden age has ended. I do not cite in evidence President William Routh's sixty-four years as president of Magdalen College, Oxford, early in the nineteenth century; to be appointed at the age of thirty-six and die in office at the age of a hundred is not a usual basis for a career. Mark Hopkins's thirty-six years at Williams College in the nineteenth century was not unusual, however, and in the recent past, the presidents of Princeton and Harvard have held their posts for twenty years and more. If the job is not much fun—and deans, provosts, and vice presidents seem to enjoy the work almost as little as their heads—it is partly because the broad public seems

[152]

unwilling to give the people doing the job their whole-hearted support.

It is, of course, impossible that higher education should satisfy the complaints of all its critics. It is not shortage of money but the dictates of elementary logic that forbid us to do contradictory things simultaneously. Confronting the angriness of debate in higher education, former president of Harvard Derek Bok some years ago suggested that everyone should reflect on the problems that society had thrust at the higher education system as if they were all to be solved simultaneously, and in ways that posed no threats of mutual inconsistency. Few people listened—but Bok was quite right. It is not possible simultaneously to abandon "useless" subjects and still promote a disinterested passion for classical learning. It is not possible to insist that researchers should spend all their time in the laboratory or the library and yet teach longer hours than high school teachers do. It is not possible to discipline students so that they become respectable, polite, and unthreatening middle-class adults while respecting their rights to absolute freedom of speech. I here round up the sharpest complaints about liberal education (in the narrow sense) and about the illiberalism of many colleges and universities, and say something about their plausibility and implausibility. They can be bundled together as a single claim that nobody would quite dare to make, but that has a certain surface plausibility and certainly captures the spirit of such works as Martin Anderson's *Impostors in the Temple*.[3] In the past, well-qualified young persons attended affordable institutions of higher education where they were taught by hardworking scholars, on an agreed-upon curriculum constructed on agreed-upon principles, in an atmosphere of mutual toleration and respect that both reflected and reinforced the commitment of faculty and students alike to the central values of Western civilization. Today, all manner of unqualified persons, assisted by dubious schemes of affirmative action, attend institutions that charge excessive amounts of money for the inattentive and reluctant efforts of professors who construct eccentric courses, based on no visible principle beyond the accommodation of assorted culturally separatist groups ranging from angry lesbians to angry African Americans.

Academic Freedom

I begin with the most damaging suggestion, that universities and colleges have renounced their commitment to freedom of speech and inquiry. If it were true that they had done so, it might not be wholly disastrous for liberal education in the narrowest sense: we have agreed that a liberal education in the old-fashioned sense of a non-vocational education rich in classics, literature, and history could be transmitted without much concern for the values of a liberal society. It was what Yale, Princeton, and Harvard did in the eighteenth century, and did in the interests of a not particularly liberal Protestantism. It would, however, be the death of any claim to be places that served the wider society by helping young people to become better citizens of a liberal society by teaching them toleration, open-mindedness, and an ability to argue for their own views without resorting to coercive measures.

IS HIGHER EDUCATION A FRAUD?

It is important to be clear about the nature of universities' and colleges' special and peculiar concern with free speech. There is a temptation to think that the United States is committed to "absolute" freedom of speech, protected by the First Amendment. That is simply wrong. There is no absolute right of free speech, either inside or outside a university: pleading that you were using "speech" and are protected by the First Amendment would do you no good if you were charged with blackmail, fraud, or slander. As Mill observed in *On Liberty*, we must not go into the street and hold up a placard announcing "Corn Dealers Are Thieves" before an angry mob intent on burning down a corn merchant's house.[4] Nor is the famous right to teach whatever we think proper—the *Lehrfreiheit* that German professors insisted on—to be taken as an absolute right to say whatever we like. If I am hired to teach the philosophy of Plato but tell my class my eccentric views on thermodynamics instead, I shall rightly get the sack and no court will help me. Professorial freedom is in essence a guild privilege; within our competence, and as long as we fulfill our contractual obligations, nobody else may tell us how to do our job. The right to this freedom stems not from a general First Amendment principle but from the nature of the job. German students had their own "professional" freedom—*Lernfreiheit*, or the right to study what they chose. As the fact that these freedoms coexisted in Germany with the authoritarian institutions of the new and assertive Empire might suggest, these freedoms, too, had nothing to do with First Amendment rights, though they naturally attracted American reformers a hundred years ago who wanted to get away from a prescribed and uniform curriculum, and to be protected from the whims of presidents and trustees.

The complicated situations arise when we wish to teach potentially contentious subjects. It is no accident that American concern with academic freedom began at the end of the last century when Leland Stanford's widow demanded that the president of Stanford University should sack the economist E. A. Ross. Ross was an ardent opponent of the gold standard and made many speeches supporting the populist Democrat William Jennings Bryan in his campaign for using both gold and silver as the monetary standard. His greater offense, however, was to urge that no more Chinese migrant workers should be allowed into California, and then to suggest that natural monopolies such as railroads should be taken into public ownership. Leland Stanford had made his money from railroads built with coolie labor. Ross was sacked, but, unusually for the times, he put up a fight about it and was supported by the American Economics Association. Fifteen years later, in 1915, the American Association of University Professors was founded to defend professors against repressive administrators and donors; its Committee A has been doing so ever since. The history of the defense of free speech within the university has until very recently been one of left-wing academics under fire from right-wing outside forces. This is not the place to rehearse the history of McCarthyism in the 1950s, but in those years several hundred people lost their jobs because they either had been or were suspected of being members of the Communist Party, or because they refused in a high-minded way to swear loyalty oaths or denounce their friends and colleagues.

IS HIGHER EDUCATION A FRAUD?

The novelty of the present situation is that the threat to freedom comes, or is widely thought to come, from within the academy and from people who believe themselves to be radicals rather than conservatives. That the left is not always on the side of free speech is not news: Lenin famously observed, "We seek freedom for the truth, not for error," and the left has often enough taken that view. The present situation is not that of a Leninist takeover, however, and former leftists are often as unhappy as anyone else about the contemporary scene. There are two common complaints. One is that assorted forms of "post-modernist" skepticism have induced in teachers and their students a wholesale contempt for the truth; if we can "really" take free speech seriously only if we take seriously the thought that universities perform what Dewey in 1902 called "the truth function," it is less likely that we shall take freedom seriously if we have become skeptical about truth. Professor Richard Rorty has argued against this, and to my mind conclusively. According to Rorty's account of the controversy, it is not truth in the everyday sense that post-modernists are skeptical about—post-modernists do not propose to walk out of high windows on the grounds that gravitation is a figment of the imagination or an upper-class scheme to diminish the ambitions of the working class; rather, it is the concept of Truth—the thought that there is a fixed body of special truths, truths that everyone can and should grasp, and, above all, truths that are mirrored by our best account of them—about which we should be skeptical. Dewey was skeptical about Truth when he announced that the university's function was the truth function. This is, however, a philosophical skepticism about theories of truth; from it, nothing at all follows about such humdrum matters as whether it is better to trust a trained physicist than your local mail carrier if you wish to learn about physics, just as you'd be better off to trust the mail carrier's directions to a nearby house.

But Rorty is a staunch defender of academic freedom. His argument in a nutshell is that there is almost no philosophical argument that deserves as much credence as the proposition that we should preserve academic freedom in the face of everything except dire and immediate emergency. Not everyone is persuaded. Nor are the unpersuaded uniformly on the opposite side of the political spectrum from Rorty. It is difficult to reconcile our ordinary, intuitive sense that truth is something we search for, and something we cannot tinker with to suit our own purposes, with the pragmatist view that "truth" is a label we attach to statements we find useful. Russell, after all, was a radical of much the same sort as Dewey, and found Dewey's pragmatism "impious." One may suspect that Rorty's critics find his pragmatism impious today. Nonetheless, it is clear enough that nothing at all follows about academic freedom from our espousing an objectivist or a pragmatist view of truth. Generations of critics have argued that it is just because Plato thought that the truth was intuited infallibly by the philosophers to whom it was vouchsafed that Plato was contemptuous of all forms of freedom and freedom of inquiry most of all.

The more interesting complaint is that it is an excess of kindness that has destroyed academic freedom. We have moved on from the perfectly proper thought that students ought to be provided with a learning environment that is friendly, that does not expose them to humiliation, and that allows them to build up their self-confidence as they learn to the utterly destructive thought that teachers must police their thoughts and words in order to avoid causing pain *no matter what*. Jonathan Rauch's *Kindly Inquisitors* is an instance of this kind of complaint.[5] Rauch agrees that kindness is in its place a considerable virtue. Intellectual life, however, depends on our tolerating a large measure of unkindness—especially unkindness to those in authority. But learning to endure disagreement is something students have to do, too. None of us enjoys having our views of the world overturned or even questioned, and the temptation to silence our critics is a permanent one. The Soviet geneticist Trofim Lysenko could call on the resources of the Stalinist state to ensure that his Lamarckian ideas about evolution were not challenged, but American scientists, too, have been known to bully their inferiors into producing falsified results. The history of most intellectual inquiry is full of persons in authority imposing their views on the powerless; the oddity today is that it is the powerless who have gained the upper hand.

So-called critical race theory provides an example of a well-thought-out theory that explicitly assaults academic freedom. The argument is simple. Some people—racial and sexual minorities especially—live in constant fear of humiliation. By some accounts, so great is this fear that the sufferer will hardly be able to work at all unless everyone else exercises the utmost sensitivity to his anxieties. Since critical race theorists are academic lawyers, they look to legislative measures—speech codes, the criminalization of "hate speech," and the threat of dismissal—to make teachers toe the line. There are many objections to allowing people who claim to be upset or offended dictate the terms of campus life. Not the least of them is the risk of competitive claims to victim status. When an African American expresses her sincere belief in the course of a class discussion on the legal regulation of sexual conduct that homosexuals are sick, and a classmate complains to the dean of students, are we to endanger the African American's self-esteem by sending her off for sensitivity training or the self-esteem of the gay complainant by providing no redress? It is no laughing matter. Quite apart from the simple misery caused to students or faculty who are hauled up in front of disciplinary panels or, in extreme cases, dismissed, a student's subsequent career can be blighted by such charges even if they are not sustained.

The intellectual objection is still simpler. If we think we ought not to pain people who hold different views from ours, we get such nonsense as the view that creationism ought to be taught alongside real science because those who believe in creationism might get distressed if their worldview is ignored. As a recipe for turning the citizens of some states, if not the entire population of the United States, into scientific illiterates, it can hardly be beaten. The moral is an old one: people who can't stand the heat should stay out of the kitchen. If you don't like having your beliefs questioned, don't go to college. This is infinitely far from suggesting that either students or faculty can rightly say or do whatever they choose in the classroom. If I am hired to teach calculus, it is my job to try to teach *everybody* who turns up. If students are idle or disorganized, it may also be my job to send them away until such time as they can

[160]

put their minds to the task in hand. If they are not idle or disorganized, and I still find it hard to teach them, it is my task to work out ways of improving things. It is absolutely right for a college to bend its collective intelligence to the question of how to make the classroom a welcoming rather than a forbidding environment, and there is a perfectly proper kind of sensitivity training that consists in persuading faculty—and students—to pay attention to the way their teaching habits and classroom practices draw in or shut out particular students. But that is very different from allowing the offended to dictate what may and may not be discussed.

Stanley Fish's entertaining and duplicitous little tract *There's No Such Thing as Free Speech (And It's a Good Thing, Too)* caused great offense a few years ago—especially to those who read no further than the title. But just as Professor Rorty wishes universities to prefer truth to falsehood while insisting that there is no such thing as the Truth, so Professor Fish wishes universities to prefer freedom to comfort while insisting that there is no such *thing* as free speech. To which one can only reply, whoever supposed there was? More interestingly, Professor Fish tried to persuade his readers to get out of the habit of contrasting the classroom devoted to free inquiry with the "politicized" classroom. Unfortunately, he once again did so in a fashion calculated to arouse resistance rather than assent, by insisting that all arguments about silencing and censorship are political arguments about who can talk about what, where, and how. However, he was essentially right to insist that what we conventionally describe as academic freedom is itself a political achievement. Liberal societies have made a "political" decision that there should be places where argument flourishes and where the chips fall where they may. It is a political choice to stick up for the principle that within the walls of a classroom the only constraints on what can be said are those dictated by a concern to get at the truth. Insult and abuse are out; politics in the narrow, everyday sense should have no hand in constraining the conversation. The greatest threat to freedom within the classroom at present is, happily, the ordinary human frailty of people who teach for a living; we become so used to telling students what to think that we forget to listen to them.

Idleness

Complaints directed against what professors do when they are working have coincided with complaints that they do no real work in the first place. Charles Sykes's *ProfScam* is the most famous example of this indictment.[6] The basis of the charge is clear enough; most professors are required to teach six or nine hours a week. Some of them are paid over $100,000 for so doing. Colleges and universities operate for about forty weeks a year, of which the teaching year occupies perhaps thirty weeks. A little mathematics yields the result that some of us earn four hundred dollars an hour at the podium; indeed, in a top-flight research university where faculty often teach only three courses a year, the sum reaches $1,000 per contact hour. It is not surprising that outsiders have thought that it sure beats working for a living. Before I explain why this is a silly way of looking at the matter, it ought to be said that very few people are in the happy position of teaching one or two three-hour courses a week. The more typical academic is teaching four or five classes a week, year in, year out, and doing it for not much more than $30,000 a year. Worse yet, a lot of such teaching is done by adjuncts who are paid $1,000 or $1,500 for a fifteen-week course, no health or pension benefits, no office, and no compensation for the work of grading and course preparation. These so-called gypsies are by anybody's standards underpaid and over-worked.

Whenever investigators have looked into the working hours of faculty, they turn out to be longer than readers of *ProfScam* would imagine. Both in the United States and Britain, most respondents say they spend between fifty and fifty-five hours a week on academic activities. It is not only that nobody in their right mind would wish to deliver an absolutely unprepared lecture; there is a great deal of other preparation required. Students and libraries need reading lists; reading lists do not create themselves, and few of us entirely like it emerging that we have put on the reading list books and journal articles that we have never looked at ourselves. Students' work needs grading; the puzzled have to be seen for long periods to restore their confidence and remove their puzzlement. Departments make other demands on their members; universities and colleges are not immune from the general rule that if we do not practice self-government, we shall be governed autocratically; and the sad truth that all radicals and insurrectionaries have discovered is that self-government is not government by mass meeting but government by committee. Even those radical democrats, the Athenians, knew that.

ALAN RYAN

The most recent survey conducted in Oxford revealed, interestingly and surprisingly, that it was humanities faculty who spent the longest hours at work—some fifty-six hours a week versus fifty-three for their colleagues in the sciences. These are almost exactly what American faculty report. What all sides complain of, however, is that the pressures of recent years have created a conflict between devoting time to teaching and devoting it to scholarship and research, not because teaching or research have been encroaching on each other but because responding to the pressure for "accountability" has been encroaching on both. Both students and those who pay their fees—whether government in Britain or state governments, parents, and colleges themselves in the United States—have demanded not only that universities improve the teaching on offer but that they *visibly guarantee* its quality; simultaneously, those who pay for research—sometimes the same bodies—demand equally visible tokens of good value. These take time to create. In Britain, particularly, so-called Research Assessment Exercises have imposed such burdens on faculty that many of them have complained that meeting the demands of the assessment process has essentially cost every department assessed the services of a member of their faculty for the better part of two years. Since the government proposes to have such exercises every four years, this is a considerable cost.

A more serious cause for anxiety may be the mismatch between what most scholars both in the United States and in Britain want to do and what they feel obliged to do. The usual defense of the modern research university's concentration on research, and its habit of rewarding faculty who publish a lot more highly than excellent teachers, is that distinguished researchers make good teachers. But the view that there is no conflict between teaching and research is at odds with faculty sentiment. In both Britain and the United States, the great majority of faculty want to teach. In both countries, something like 75 percent want to teach much more than they wish to do original research. Yet 55 percent of respondents to a 1989 Carnegie Foundation survey said they had done original research in the past two years. The explanation is doubtless that 60 percent feel that the only way to get on in the profession is by research and publication.

Aggressive critics in the past decade have complained that a good deal of what passes for research is a waste of time and effort. It is hard at times, however, not to feel that critics such as Sykes have so rigged the argument against the academy that no defense can succeed. If faculty respond to the accusation of idleness by pointing to the hours spent on scholarship and research, they are told that their research is trivial. If they respond that by the standards of their own profession it is well thought of, they find themselves facing an argument against the standards of the profession most strikingly offered by Anderson in *Impostors in the Temple*. President Reagan ran a prosperous America with no more knowledge of economics than would fill the back of an envelope, so what is the point of doing more? Of course, there are two quite serious and interesting questions lurking beneath the invective. One is whether we can know ahead of time which pieces of research will yield genuinely interesting and worthwhile results. It would be an interesting experiment to put the confidence of lay critics such as Sykes and Anderson, and of professional politicians such as Senator William Proxmire, who have insights not shared by the academy, to the test by inviting them to stake a few thousand dollars of their own on their guesses. The other is whether we do not try to cast scholarship in the humanities too much in the mold of research in the laboratory sciences. Much humanities scholarship is genuinely not unlike extending a timeless conversation between the immortal dead and their living heirs, while rather little research in the experimental sciences is anything of the sort. Humanities research might be done better if it were done more confidently.

If more make-weight research is done than is comfortable, it is because tenure and promotion arouse great anxiety and can cause considerable trouble and misery to colleagues and their employers. Most institutions therefore want an "objective" test of professorial worth; the temptation is almost irresistible to measure academic worth by weighing the quantity of publication, intuitively adjusted for the journals in which it appears or the presses who publish it. Since quality rankings are established by asking academics which journals and presses they regard as the best, they are essentially self-perpetuating, and the effect is to enforce a rather monotonous respectability as the norm. To put it otherwise, *wickedness* is much less prevalent than critics suppose; dullness rather more so.

Intellectual Disorder

Ten years ago, a conference paper by Eve Kosofsky Sedgwick, "Jane Austen and the Masturbating Girl," became the most famous paper in modern literary criticism. A *Wall Street Journal* reporter picked up the title from a Modern Language Association Conference program, and (universally unread) it became an icon for conservatives. The paper— and once they had read it, many of the critics who had been outraged by the title found it interesting—pursued a theme that is hardly a new one in literary criticism, namely the buried sexual attachments and tensions that give fiction its engrossing and sometimes disturbing effect. The novels of Henry James have attracted such attention for many years. However, the sensationalist title of Professor Sedgwick's paper became for conservative critics an emblem of the urge to demolish our cultural tradition that conservatives have detected in departments of literature all over the country. In conservative eyes, the "deconstructionist" urge is an affront to the literary tradition in which generations have been brought up. In some form, these arguments have been going on a very long time. Radicals long ago denounced the very idea of high culture as part of the ideological weaponry of the possessing classes. The interest of recent arguments is largely that late-twentieth-century radicalism has been sexual and racial rather than economic; texts have been analyzed to reveal the secrets of male oppression and female resentment more commonly than they have been analyzed to reveal the secrets of class oppression and resistance. Class, race, and gender have been the Holy Trinity of radical readers, but the last two members of the trio have been much more salient than the first. The complaints of conservative critics have been diverse. But chief among them has been the complaint that the moral lessons that literature can convey have been slighted for political purposes. The oddity of this complaint is twofold, first because the conservative case is duplicitous, since it is inspired by a different politics but a politics nonetheless, and second because both sides share the same, highly implausible, faith in the therapeutic power of literature—if it is read in the right way.

Debates over high culture become ugly when high culture is invested with religious or therapeutic qualities. The view that there is (or ought to be) a "canon" of great works whose acquaintance will yield students a form of secular redemption has been a great distraction; it inspires foolish arguments about what is in and what is out, and incites young people who ought to know better to think that if much talk of a canon is superstitious, so is all talk of better and worse. It is also an odd commentary on our forgetfulness. A hundred years ago, critics complained that a real religious allegiance was being sacrificed to literary studies. Today, conservative critics of modern high education write as though literary studies were itself a branch of a religious education. If we ceased to think that a proper understanding of the Great Books (whichever they might be) is redemptive, there'd be less temptation to take them down a peg or two and insist on their all too human origins. If we treat a literary education as tantamount to induction into the true faith, we must expect incivility. Defenders of the faith have never treated heretics kindly, and religious insurgents have rarely been polite about the establishment.

The implausibility of the entire system of higher education being implicated in a campaign to undermine Western culture is obvious enough. It is worth recalling the figures this chapter began with: 2.6 percent of all students major in English. Almost as many major in catering, domestic science, and hotel management. It may or may not be a good thing to teach young persons the art of portion control, or to give them diplomas in the wiles of advertising, but such students are not exactly being turned against Western civilization. They are being so thoroughly trained to take their place in the modern consumer society that a respectful skepticism about Western civilization would do them good. Perhaps the one thing on which the radicals and their critics can—or at any rate should—agree is that professional training is not enough for the whole of life. It is not exactly news that Harvard M.B.A.s have been known to commit fraud, to throw their workers onto the street needlessly, to sacrifice production to financial manipulation, and in general to behave as badly as Veblen complained that financiers behaved a hundred years ago. If they behave badly because they have been badly trained, what they lack is not a training in fancy analytical techniques but a sense of the duties of the powerful and the clever to the less powerful and the less clever.

There is perhaps, therefore, a case for insisting that everyone should take a program of general studies focused on history, literature, philosophy, and science, either in the final year of high school or as a foundation in the undergraduate college. I have some doubt whether colleges and universities can do very much to instill virtues that parents have failed to instill, but it is possible that they can do something to get students to perceive the implications of the moral ideals they have acquired. It would at the very least do something to reduce the number of young people who appear to live wholly solipsistically, utterly unanchored in their own time and place. Whether there is a public for such a program is another matter. Those of us who would like every student to be equipped with the adult version of what E. D. Hirsch baptized as "cultural literacy" will inevitably confront those who insist that students should focus on whatever they want to, whether in the name of choice or so that they can specialize in what they are good at. Bliss Carnochan's engaging little book *The Battleground of the Curriculum* reminds us that the fight for and against the "elective" system began a hundred-odd years ago with a knockdown fight between Presidents Charles W. Eliot of Harvard and James McCosh of Princeton. Eliot, a chemist and a reformer who had seen and admired the German research universities of the 1860s, saw no reason why students should not assemble their own degree schemes out of whatever the university provided; McCosh, the irascible Scots Presbyterian philosopher and scourge of J. S. Mill, was equally sure that no man could call himself educated who did not have a sufficient diet of Latin, Greek, divinity, moral philosophy, history, and literature. We still fight about Cafeteria versus Core, and in the name of the same values.

Failed attempts to provide a blueprint for general education seem to suffer from one of two different afflictions: either they are geared to transitory purposes, or they confuse general principles with their particular implementation. President James Conant's postwar scheme embodied in the Harvard Red Book was too narrowly focused on the need to boost American self-confidence in the competition with the Soviet Union—although it has been described as a plan that was immensely influential everywhere except at

Harvard. The Great Books curricula that St. John's, Annapolis, and its sister colleges have implemented remain a minority taste because most students and teachers think they have made a fetish of studying original texts. The truth is that as between *War and Peace* and *Don Quixote* it may not matter which one is studied so long as the student learns how to get inside the imaginative world of Tolstoy or Cervantes, to explore it with patience and thought, and to derive pleasure from interacting with the intelligence of a great writer.

As always, the threat to liberal education comes mainly from the desire to make higher education useful, that is, from the desire to give people degrees in vocational subjects. In a rational world, we might be able to separate out two sorts of higher education without insulting either, and allow one of them to give a V.A.B.—a baccalaureate in vocational arts; in the United States and Britain at any rate, "credentialism" rules. People who would receive vocational qualifications do not want what the world will not label "degrees," and they are right to suspect that there would always be a difference in esteem, acceptability to employers, and the recruitment of faculty to teach these programs. Yet the idea that what makes a vocational training eligible for degree status is a component of liberal education is resisted for plausible reasons. Engineering degrees take students five years to acquire; are we to add another eighteen months to civilize our engineers? It is not obvious that the answer is no, though it is not obvious that engineering school is the best place to provide such an education. Given the diversity of courses offered in the 3,400 colleges and universities in the United States, it is not surprising that critics complain that the system does a bad job of promoting high culture and liberal values. They are right, but the prior question is whether we should expect it to do so—let alone whether we should expect *all* of it to do so. Still, the point remains that when all the sound and fury over the so-called culture wars dies away, the answer to the question of what most threatens liberal education in American colleges is business studies and vocational education.

Utopia(s)

There are two familiar complaints against higher education that I have as yet said nothing about. One is the complaint that it has become absurdly expensive to attend the best universities and colleges—although this is a complaint most obviously leveled at private schools, the out-of-state cost of education at good state universities is only a little less alarming. If Princeton will today set you back $30,000 a year for tuition, room, board, and books, the University of Michigan will cost an out-of-state student $24,000. The second is the complaint that where intellectual standards haven't been rotted by post-modernism and literary radicalism, they have succumbed to the pressures of affirmative action and multiculturalism.

The cost of higher education is appalling—I say this the more readily as a parent who is suffering its expensiveness. It is not only expensive, but has for the past twenty-five years become more expensive at twice the general rate of inflation. The cause is not the greed of professors, whose salaries have only barely kept pace with inflation—unlike those of doctors and lawyers, which have risen very much faster. Part of the explanation is the costliness of laboratory science; part is the costliness of new telephone, computer, and similar infrastructure. And part, alas, is the expense of adding administrators to comply with the needs of regulators and others, to provide a sort of student-welfare state. Not unlike medicine, where increasingly complicated apparatuses and increasingly complicated underpinnings of helpers have pushed up costs, higher education finds it impossible to improve productivity without lowering quality.

The deeper puzzle is why the consumers tolerate the fact that so much of higher education is no more than remedial secondary education. It is very extravagant to send students to university to do in four years what they could easily do in three, or to spend four years reaching only the level of the B.A. when they could easily reach a notch higher. Adequate secondary education would cost a fifth or a quarter of what higher education costs to achieve the same results, and would allow colleges and universities to teach to a proper level. I am baffled by the lack of pressure to do it. Year after year we are told that there will be a revolt against high tuition fees, and that public universities face taxpayer revolts, but nothing actually happens. When President Bill Clinton offers to give students $1,500 a year to pay for two years of community college after high school, nobody laughs—but the only sensible response is to ask why students should receive a thirteenth- and fourteenth-grade education when they haven't had an eighth-grade education already. Princeton was recently spending more than $45,000 per year per student, and yet regards it as tolerable to teach elementary-level foreign languages to freshmen students. It plainly isn't. It is a waste of money. Of course, students might need to acquire a second or third foreign language during their time at university, but there, too, it is not obvious that picking up useful skills should count toward a degree in the same way as the subjects studied once we have those skills, let alone that the skills should be imparted so expensively.

Multiculturalism

Issues of affirmative action on the one hand and multiculturalism on the other need a book rather than a few paragraphs to resolve. Still, the general principles that should animate liberals are not complicated. There is a proper place for affirmative action within a meritocratic framework, and in the light of liberal values. If universities and colleges believe that they can detect genuine but untapped—or not fully tapped—ability, they should give the bearers of that ability a chance to realize it. And if such students face other obstacles to success than the simpler forms of missing opportunity—such as having been to schools that could not teach calculus, or that could not offer Advanced Placement classes—we should try to remove those obstacles up to the point where doing so threatens to disadvantage other students or wreck the institutions to which access is being sought. Making the point more concrete, Harvard and Princeton among many other schools run pre-matriculation seminars for minority students to bring them up to speed in essay writing and research skills. Such students do not, even then, graduate at quite the rate of their white peers—but they have a graduation rate of 85 percent against 95 percent, which compares rather favorably with a national average of barely 50 percent for students of all races. As I said in the introduction, affirmative action as we usually understand it is essentially a palliative; true affirmative action would begin long before children reached kindergarten and would end long after they left college. Without a stable family background, children cannot learn; without jobs to go to, students will not learn. Looking for underexercised talent is what all teachers try to do.

As to multiculturalism, the truth is simple, but almost universally resisted. There is only one culture, and all of it is "our" culture. It comes in innumerable tongues and styles, attached to innumerable peoples and societies, but in principle it is open to anyone who can acquire the needed language and contextual knowledge. I do not wish to beg the question of who "we" are, nor to imply that anyone's attitude toward that culture should be reverential. We may argue endlessly about who we are, and we ought to understand the price at which the greatest cultural achievements have been purchased. It may or may not have been necessary for there to be slaves in Athens for Plato and Aristotle to have leisure to think; but both of them thought it was.[8] Nor did they flinch at what slavery meant for the slave. They knew that to be a pedagogue in a well-run and affluent household was usually a good job; to work in the silver mines at Laurium was a death sentence. The views of Plato and Aristotle on slavery and the material foundation of the culture they graced do not discredit their philosophy, but they surely ought to induce a wincing realization that not all good things turn up together and mutually support one another.

In his somewhat flat-footed way, Dewey got it right in 1916 in his little essay "Nationalizing Education,"[9] in which he argued that good hyphens connected while bad hyphens separated. Certainly, we cannot embark on the exploration of human culture without starting from somewhere in particular; African Americans will have a different starting point from many white Americans, but this ought to be the starting point for a conversation about the contributions that different peoples and societies have made to a common culture—and common not in the sense that we all hold the same view of it as that we can all make our own use of it. The alternative is just a retreat from what the world has to offer, and a narrowing of possibility.

If one says that the point of education is to allow students to become fully the heirs of our culture, almost anyone will ask, who is this we? The reply, of course, is that we are many, our culture is plural, and that is a good thing. Multiculturalism is not a threat to the unity of the American republic but a reflection of the facts of life. The peoples of the North Atlantic have become a comparative and historical people, and the British and the Americans perhaps most strikingly so—though the Dutch and the Danes might have a different view; we might once not have been so open to the world, and we might wish we hadn't become so, but we are. The United States is a peculiarly multicultural society, but the European high culture that the anti-multiculturalists affect to admire is itself many, not one: it comes in national and subnational varieties, and it is only describable against a background of contrasting alternatives—European pop culture; the folk cultures of pre-industrial, non-class societies; non-European culture, whatever it might be.

Any education that makes people less interested in another society's vision of the world has gone badly wrong. Any student decently taught and allowed to look at the world will be curious about what happens beyond his or her front door. Indefensible multiculturalism is not multiculturalism at all but a rearguard attempt to protect cherished beliefs by forbidding one's children, one's ethnic group, or one's co-cultists to discover that there are alternatives to the local prejudices. This is monoculturalism practiced at the expense of the innocent, and the reverse of everything that the idea of liberal education stands for. It is fashionable to sneer at the wilder excesses of Afrocentric education, but parochial schools, ecclesiastically controlled universities, and the followers of the Lubavitcher Rebbe exemplify in their own perhaps less flamboyant fashion most of the same vices.

In principle and in general, the old view is right that liberal education is multicultural in intention—music is anybody's music, philosophy is anyone's truth. This is not cultural imperialism under another label; where there is more or less objective truth to be had, it is not "Western" or "European" or "American" science that prevails, but good science over less good. Where there is not, there is no reason of principle why Western composers can't embrace Balinese music, why Japanese students cannot enjoy Shakespeare, why British political theorists cannot appreciate Chinese political thinkers of two and a half millennia ago. Time, familiarity, linguistic competence, and a whole lot else make it hard to become multiply fluent. One reason for hope is that so many young people do a rather good job of becoming so. *Nihil humanum mihi alienum puto* has always been a good liberal motto: intellectual freedom is the freedom that comes of the sense that we are possessed of all human culture.

Let me end by suggesting four things that matter very much. Not all institutions can do all of them, and not every student benefits from each of them. But if we were sure that the higher education system could attend to all of them, we should have every reason to be happy. To start at the utilitarian end, the absence of good vocational training for sixteen- to nineteen-year-olds is a scandal. The English-speaking countries seem to be worse at this than Scandinavia and Germany, but whatever the reason for that, good post-sixteen vocational education would do an enormous amount of good. We cannot be sure by the time students are fourteen or fifteen that they will *never* have any great interest in academic subjects. Still, we can probably tell that they won't be turned on by academic matters in the next half dozen years, and the students of whom that's true would be better off being taught how to become effective workers. This is not a question of training them to be manual workers, since the number of those that society can employ is very small and is going to go on dropping; but the line between supervising processes that are largely carried out by automated machinery and skilled manual labor is very thin. What is needed is training that provides generalizable skills. This would require a lot of humanities teaching. The inculcation of general knowledge about a mobile society may be one of the best vocational skills we could pass on; if people have to change jobs three or four times in a lifetime, they need a social fluency and imaginativeness that we don't ordinarily think of as job skills but which plainly are.

A second thing we ought to welcome is the pursuit of difficulty. Many things in life are wonderful because they are very difficult as well as being beautiful or interesting or useful, too. Among these are the ballet, playing the solo trumpet as well as Miles Davis or Wynton Marsalis, and being able to illuminate a play or a novel in the way some literary critics can. They are skills whose exercise leaves the spectator slightly breathless. Good physicists got that sort of frisson from the work of Richard Feynman. I have had half a dozen students in the course of thirty years whose swiftness and acuteness of understanding have done the same to me. Students study philosophy in part for the sake of the pleasure of seeing people vastly cleverer than themselves engaging with issues that it has taken every intellectual skill they possess to get clear and to see into. To describe Kant's *Critique of Pure Reason* as a source of pleasure perhaps ought to be avoided, since many students have found it utterly intractable; but if there is pleasure to be had from hanging off a rock face, as there clearly is, there is a pleasure of a not dissimilar kind from venturing a view on what Immanuel Kant's equally vertiginous derivation of the laws of the human mind may have been about.

One task of the university or college is thus to let students see if this is what they enjoy. Another is honesty about the fact that many will not enjoy it, honesty in admitting that getting one's skills up to scratch is sometimes boring, that the discovery of the limits of one's aptitudes

ALAN RYAN

can be painful and depressing; but one of the few claims
to special standing that universities and colleges can decently make is that we offer such encounters with intellectual difficulty, both in research work and for undergraduates. The wickedness of grade inflation on the one hand
and overcertification on the other is that they encourage
people to suppose that nothing ought to be difficult,
whereas it is one of the peculiarities of human beings that
they want difficulty—a truth we admit in the context of
sports, but somehow not elsewhere. Students who are ready
to spend five hours a day practicing for the swim team
ought to be quicker than they usually are to acknowledge
that it may take much longer than that to come to terms
with Hume or Plato or Gerard Manley Hopkins.

A third task is that of ensuring not only that students
can express themselves but that they have a clear sense of
what it is that they wish to express. One of the very few
depressing aspects of teaching my exceedingly clever,
friendly, and diligent students at Princeton was the inability of so many of them to write in a way that gave
either themselves or anyone else much pleasure. Of course,
many wrote decently, and some wrote very well. But 50
percent of my students were essentially tone-deaf to their
native language, and 20 percent were quite unable to write
in such a way that what they said was mirrored interestingly in the way they said it. Asked to write a paragraph
of "Hobbesian" argument, they were baffled. Perhaps
worse, they would have had no idea how it was that the
way Hobbes wrote and what Hobbes had to say were so
intimately connected that it takes some skill to rephrase
Hobbes's ideas without losing their sense entirely. The

point, of course, is that *mere* self-expression is of no interest unless one has something to express; knowing what that is is the first step in criticism. It cannot be learned without mastering the art of writing in many styles. That is the one and only way in which Matthew Arnold's defense of the priority of literature over science in a liberal education has some cogency. A liberally educated physicist, of whom there are happily many, knows not only what the glories of the discipline are, but how to strike a spark when explaining them; that needs a critical intelligence more literary than scientific. The late Richard Feynman was not only a Nobel prize–winning physicist but a writer able to offer readers some degree of intimacy with the life of that Rolls-Royce among minds. He may well have thought of himself—outside subatomic physics—as a superior jester, but the extraordinary elegance of his intelligence emerged in a natural elegance of literary style.

Finally, I revert to the thought that I began with. One of the central purposes of education is to overcome the sense of being "thrown" into a meaningless world. Anyone who wants to connect liberalism as a set of cultural and political ambitions with liberal education as a commitment to a humanist and historical understanding of human culture hopes that the second will sustain the first and that the first will provide a proper shelter for the second. What that means is that multiculturalism is an unforced enthusiasm for exploring the variety of human invention and experience, not a reluctant concession to anxiety and aggression or a mere parceling out of scarce jobs. Affirmative action is a natural outgrowth of the conviction that just about anybody will, with a fair start and in a welcoming environment, wish to and be able to become an active citizen of a global intellectual and cultural community. A humanist education is indispensable because the past contains the cultural capital of humanity; and a scientific education is indispensable both because the scientific exploration of the world is one of the glories of humanity and because what "science" is, in the end, is no more than knowledge that we think reliable.

This short way with multiculturalism—about which I am wholly in earnest—runs into some familiar complaints from feminist and non-Western critics. Arguments for traditional liberal education have been disparaged as obsessively concerned with Dead White European Males. There is enough in the complaint to make it improper glibly to dismiss it by replying that we can hardly concentrate on unborn women of color. It is certainly the case that claims have been made for the virtues of the works that compose the tradition that a humanist education is concerned with that nobody can take seriously. Still, the unhappy fact remains that we cannot study what has not been created. Historical and literary disciplines must concentrate their attention on work that actually exists. Until the nineteenth century, few past societies offered much scope to women who wished to write, paint, create sculptures, or practice as architects, let alone become philosophers or scientists. We may lament that there were few mathematicians to equal Aspasia and few poets to equal Sappho, but we cannot invent a past that did not happen or pretend to find second-rate work better than it is because it was done by a woman. It is hard to think of Mary Astell as a political thinker on a par with Hobbes. Indeed, to do so would be to add the insult of condescension in our generation to the injury of exclusion in the past.

Other critics have thought that the defense of a liberal and humanist education was no better than an imperialist attempt to impose modern Western values on the rest of the world. This is a complaint that is usually greeted with an affected incomprehension. It might be better to agree that to some degree the concern for liberal education is imperialist—but not because it is a form of intellectual terrorism, and not because it imposes anything on anybody. It is imperialist in the sense that all liberal ideals are imperialist; because they are supposed to appeal to any rational person who takes time to consider them, those who are attached to them believe that everyone else ought to be attached to them, too. They are universalist rather than particularist in their scope; liberals are therefore more inclined than most to see differences of language and geography as something to be overcome rather than to be taken as setting the boundaries of comprehension and enjoyment. This is true, even of those liberals who are most eloquent in insisting on the importance of the "small platoons" to which we feel most intimately attached. Most liberals believe—even if they only admit it somewhat blushingly —that the processes of economic and scientific modernization will bring all or almost all societies to a liberal, egalitarian, secular view of politics and culture and therefore of education, and that given a clear field a local version of a liberal society will secure the loyalties and affections of its inhabitants. Needless to say, anyone who believes this, in the teeth of the horrors of the twentieth century, the resurgence of religious fundamentalism in the West as well as elsewhere, and the vitality of a conservative tradition that regards a faith in progress as foolishness, must temper hope with anxiety—but they ought also to temper anxiety with hope.

NOTES

Introduction

1. *The Economist*, vol. 342, no. 8010 (March 29–April 4, 1997), pp. 25–27.
2. Christopher J. Lucas, *American Higher Education* (New York, 1994), p. xi.
3. E. D. Hirsch, *Cultural Literacy: What Every American Needs to Know* (New York, 1987); *The Schools We Need: And Why We Don't Have Them* (New York, 1996).
4. Jonathan Kozol, *Illiterate America* (New York, 1985), p. 4.
5. Theodore Sizer, *Horace's Hope* (New York, 1996), p. xvi.
6. Ibid.
7. *Time*, vol. 149, no. 5 (March 7, 1997).
8. Seymour Martin Lipset, *American Exceptionalism* (New York, 1995).
9. Benjamin Barber, *An Aristocracy of Everyone* (New York, 1992).
10. John Dewey, "Dewey Outlines Utopian Schools," *Later Works*, vol. 9 (Carbondale, Ill., 1986), p. 136.

NOTES

Chapter 1

1. Charles Murray and Richard J. Herrnstein, *The Bell Curve* (New York, 1994); Russell Jacoby and Naomi Glauberman, eds., *The Bell Curve Debate* (New York, 1995).
2. Michael Young, *The Rise of the Meritocracy* (Harmondsworth, 1959).
3. Richard Hofstadter, *Anti-Intellectualism in American Life* (New York, 1963), p. 345.
4. The German title of Sigmund Freud's *Civilization and Its Discontents* (New York, 1951) could more literally have been translated as "anxiety in culture," but the sense of culture was the anthropologist's rather than Arnold's.
5. Max Weber, *The Protestant Ethic and the Spirit of Capitalism* (1904–05), (New York, 1930).
6. Bliss Carnochan, *The Battleground of the Curriculum* (New York, 1993).
7. Lucas, *American Higher Education*, p. 155ff.
8. J. S. Mill, *Considerations on Representative Government* (London, 1910), p. 261n.

Chapter 2

1. John Dewey, *Experience and Education, Later Works*, vol. 13 (Carbondale, Ill., 1986), pp. 5–15.
2. David Tyack and Larry Cuban, *Tinkering Toward Utopia* (Cambridge, 1995).

NOTES

3. Quoted in Tyack and Cuban, *Tinkering Toward Utopia*, p. 14.
4. Tyack and Cuban, *Tinkering Toward Utopia*, ch. 3.
5. Ibid., p. 21.
6. George Dykhuizen, *The Life and Mind of John Dewey* (Carbondale, Ill., 1974), p. 329.
7. Quoted in Steven Rockefeller, *John Dewey* (New York, 1991), p. 328.
8. John Dewey, "My Pedagogic Creed," *Early Works*, vol. 5 (Carbondale, Ill., 1978), pp. 94–95.
9. Sidney Hook, *Out of Step* (New York, 1987), pp. 82–83.
10. John Dewey, *How We Think, Middle Works*, vol. 6 (Carbondale. Ill., 1985), pp. 237–38.
11. John Dewey, "Dewey Outlines Utopian Schools," *Later Works*, vol. 9 (Carbondale, Ill., 1986), p. 136.

Chapter 3

1. Lucas, *American Higher Education*, p. 227; see also Francis Oakley, *Community of Learning* (New York, 1992), from which most of the data here are taken.
2. Robert M. Hutchins, *The Higher Learning in America* (New York, 1936), p. 66.
3. Martin Anderson, *Impostors in the Temple* (New York, 1993).
4. J. S. Mill, *On Liberty* (London, 1910), p. 114.
5. Jonathan Rauch, *Kindly Inquisitors* (New York, 1990).
6. Charles Sykes, *ProfScam* (New York, 1989).

7. Carnochan, *Battleground*, pp. 13–17.

8. Aristotle, *Politics*, tr. Ernest Barker (Oxford, 1949), bk. I, sec. 8.

9. John Dewey, "Nationalizing Education," *Middle Works*, vol. 10 (Carbondale, Ill., 1985), pp. 202–15.

INDEX

INDEX

INDEX

INDEX

INDEX

frontier, American, 64

fundamentalism, religious, 12, 52

Germany: secondary education in,
49, 124; social values of, 22;
universities in, 77, 81–82,
92–93, 155, 170

Gilman, Daniel, 82

Giuliani, Rudolph, 19

Glasgow, University of, 66

Godwin, William, 46

grade inflation, 180

graduate education, 81–82, 106,
150; growth of, 147

Great Books, 151, 168, 171

Greeks, ancient, 40, 61, 91, 125,
175

Haileybury College (London),
60

Hall, G. S., 82

Handsworth (England), 20

Harpur, William Rainey, 110

Harvard University, 8, 13, 83,
102, 145, 151–53, 169, 171,
174; affirmative action at, 174;
history of, 62, 63, 74, 77, 82,
154, 170

Head Start program, 139

Hegel, G.W.F., 54, 127

Heidelberg, University of, 82

Herbart, Johann, 127, 128

Herzog (Bellow), 53

high culture, debates over, 167–
68

higher education, 26, 143–84;
for blacks, 83–84; cost of,
172–73; culture wars in, 36–
37, 166–72; general studies
requirements in, 169–71;
graduate, *see* graduate education; growth of, 146–49; high
school and, 106–7; Mill on,
60–61; multiculturalism in,
174–78; number of students
in, 145–46; origins of, in
U.S., 74–78; public dissatis-
faction with, 4–5, 152–54;
remedial education in, 142,
173–74; research orientation
in, 38–39, 149–51, 164–66;
threat to free speech and inquiry in, 51–52, 154–62;
traditionalist view of, 52;
underfunding of, 143–44; for
women, 82–83; working
hours of faculty in, 162–64;
see also specific institutions

Higher Learning in America, The
(Hutchins), 149, 151

Higher Learning in America, The
(Veblen), 149

high schools, 5, 26, 38, 101,
138; curriculum of, 10, 12,
106–8; inner-city, 17, 129; in
1950s, 49–50; nineteenth-
century, 80, 106; utopian,
140–42

Hirsch, E. D., 5, 32–34, 91,
104–5, 170

[193]

INDEX

INDEX

[195]

INDEX

INDEX

INDEX

INDEX

LC 1011 .R93 1998
Ryan, Alan
Liberal Anxieties and
Liberal Education.